"Megan Hill has g   1 useful and eloquent.
Many of us, mysel.   untruth about prayer:
that it should always be easy and spontaneous, free of any hint of discipline or
forethought. Megan empathetically and expressively lifts our eyes toward a higher
vision, grounded in the truth of Scripture, of prayer as a delightful duty to be
practiced, savored, and shared."

Jen Wilkin, author, *Women of the Word*; Bible study teacher

"Megan Hill moves us to pray together in our homes, communities, and churches,
offering us encouragement, experience, and counsel—all richly biblical and theological. If you and your brothers and sisters in Christ pray together with more
hope, delight, and expectancy because of reading it, I am sure that Megan will
feel her aim is realized."

J. Ligon Duncan, III, Chancellor and CEO, Reformed Theological
Seminary, Jackson, Mississippi

"When Megan Hill prays, one feels the force of an entire life spent communing
with the triune God. Now, Hill provides both the theology and practical guidance
to usher others into a rich life of prayer among fellow Christians and in corporate
worship. This book will remind you of how good and pleasant it is when God's
people dwell—and pray—together in unity."

Katelyn Beaty, Managing Editor, *Christianity Today* magazine

"Another book on prayer? Yes, and no. Yes, the focus of this book is about urgent,
corporate, sustained prayer of the kind that Scripture urges and Jesus extols as
necessary if we are to endure in the battle that faces the Christian church. And
no, for this is not just a book about prayer. Megan Hill is an accomplished author
and godly pastor's wife and mother. What she has to say comes from a sharp and
discerning mind but also from the treasury of rich pastoral experience. Could it
be that this book is God's instrument in reviving among us a healthy, vigorous,
infectious prayer life—prayer partnerships—that will redirect the course of this
world? I think it possible. I pray that it is."

Derek W. H. Thomas, Senior Minister, First Presbyterian Church,
Columbia, South Carolina; Robert Strong Professor of Systematic and
Pastoral Theology, Reformed Theological Seminary

"*Praying Together* wasn't written as a guide to improving your prayer life, but
it's impossible to read without feeling compelled to pray more often, more sin-
cerely, and with more people. Megan Hill's reverence for prayer and her personal
stories of devotion made me grateful for the gift of prayer and for a God who
uses prayer to bring us to him and to each other. *Praying Together* offers vital
encouragement."

Kate Shellnutt, Associate Editor, *Christianity Today* magazine,
Her.meneutics

"Come let us pray! A covenant child of God who learned to pray in Word and deed calls Christ's church to devoted, fervent prayer. Megan has given us a standard for kingdom praying that will bring growth and grace personally and corporately. Come, fill and disciple your hearts in remembering together who God is and what he has done. Brothers and sisters, are you ready?"

Jane Patete, Former Coordinator of Women's Ministry, the
Presbyterian Church of America

"Reading this beautiful book on prayer is like enjoying a meal with a friend. Our hostess, Megan Hill, serves the wisdom of the Word, well-baked with centuries of godly Reformed and Puritan writers and seasoned with many personal experiences. Her reflections on prayer are gentle and practical, and by God's grace I would expect you to be eager to take her recipe and use it often in your home and church."

Joel R. Beeke, President, Puritan Reformed Theological Seminary

"*Praying Together* made me want to grab a friend and pray. Megan Hill reminds us of the privilege, duty, and delight that await us as we join one another in communion with God. Weaving together the Bible's testimony about prayer and the blessing it has been to the church through the ages, this book will drive you to your knees in the anticipation of the great things God will do."

Melissa Kruger, Women's Ministry Coordinator, Uptown Church;
author, *The Envy of Eve*

"Megan Hill helps us to see, with admirable clarity and practical insight, how the triune God invites believers to gather together in prayer—in the church, in our families, and in a host of other settings. She points us to the rich promises and the remarkable blessings attending corporate prayer in Scripture. Her examples and illustrations stir us to pray with others. Read this book and join the chorus of saints lifting their voices to heaven."

Guy Prentiss Waters, James M. Baird Jr. Professor of New Testament,
Reformed Theological Seminary, Jackson, MS

"Megan Hill offers a biblical foundation as well as practical instruction for joining together to pursue an ever-deeper relationship with the Father, through the work of the Son, by the power of the Spirit. We will always find reasons not to pray together. But if we hope to live as conduits of the power of God—if we hope to feed the hungry, unbind the prisoner, comfort the grieving, and shine light in the world's dark corners—Hill encourages us to begin, together, on our knees."

Martha Manikas-Foster, Producer and Host, *Inside Out*, Family Life

"Megan Hill learned to pray as a small child in the company of her parents and members of her local church. Now she's written a rich resource on corporate prayer, helpful for families, small groups, and churches. I look forward to gathering friends and reading *Praying Together*. Better yet, I look forward to praying with them."

Jen Pollock Michel, author, *Teach Us to Want*

PRAYING TOGETHER

PRAYING TOGETHER

The Priority and Privilege of Prayer:

In Our Homes, Communities, and Churches

Megan Hill

 CROSSWAY®

WHEATON, ILLINOIS

Trade paperback ISBN: 978-1-4335-5051-5
ePub ISBN: 978-1-4335-5054-6
PDF ISBN: 978-1-4335-5052-2
Mobipocket ISBN: 978-1-4335-5053-9

Library of Congress Cataloging-in-Publication Data

Names: Hill, Megan, 1978–
Title: Praying together : the priority and privilege of prayer : in our homes, communities, and churches / Megan Hill.
Description: Wheaton : Crossway, 2016. | Includes bibliographical references and index.
Identifiers: LCCN 2015037474 | ISBN 9781433550515 (tp)
Subjects: LCSH: Prayer—Christianity.
Classification: LCC BV210.3 .H5583 2016 | DDC 248.3/2—dc23
LC record available at http://lccn.loc.gov/2015037474

Crossway is a publishing ministry of Good News Publishers.

BP		26	25	24	23	22	21	20	19	18	17	16
15	14	13	12	11	10	9	8	7	6	5	4	3	2	1

To the saints
of the Presbyterian Church of Coventry,
Hillcrest Presbyterian Church,
First Presbyterian Church, Pinehaven Presbyterian Church,
and West Springfield Covenant Community Church.
Praying together with you has been my
privilege, my duty, and my delight.

Contents

Introduction

Let's pray.

How many times have you been privileged to say or hear those words? Dietrich Bonhoeffer wrote, "It is in fact the most normal thing in the common Christian life to pray together."[1] That has been my experience. Maybe that's your story too. Like many people who grew up in a Christian home and in a gospel-proclaiming church, I learned from childhood the practice and importance of praying together in the ordinary places: our dinner table, my bedside, the church sanctuary. Early on, I internalized the Westminster Shorter Catechism's memorable definition of prayer: "Prayer is an offering up of our desires unto God, for things agreeable to his will, in the name of Christ, with confession of our sins, and thankful acknowledgement of his mercies."[2]

At the age of ten, I asked my father (a pastor) if I could join him at our church's small Wednesday night prayer meeting. On dark New England winter evenings, he and I would set out through the snow to find a group of three or five or, just maybe, seven faithful saints warming themselves in the light and heat of the church library. Mrs. Gray was always enthroned in the lone arm chair, eighty years old and occasionally nodding off, cane by her side. The rest of us sat on avocado-green vinyl chairs, dragged in from other parts of the church, cold to the touch and prone to squeaking when I wiggled.

For years I was the only child there, listening to the pre-prayer moments of discussion—Who was sick? Who was better?—and occasionally joining the subsequent hour of intercession with a feeble sentence prayer of my own. Eventually I got the idea (fresh from the pristine order of my elementary school classroom) to keep track of the requests and their divine answers. Weekly filled with a sense of responsibility, I brought my notebook and pen and studiously recorded our list of needs, sometimes going back to a previous page and gravely prompting the adults for an update. Obvious answers to our requests were few, and yet these believers were undeterred. Without a doubt, I knew by their faithful prayers that God seriously and lovingly received each petition in heaven, as I noted them in my book.

Sitting among the ordinary saints, year after year, those evenings of prayer knit my heart to Christ's church and to my God. In that church library I learned to call upon the name of the Lord in the company of his people.

Since then, praying together has become a delightful priority of first my single and then my married life. I have prayed in the church prayer meetings of five different churches, and I have prayed among the gathered church nearly every Lord's Day. Outside of the church, I've prayed with others in various parts of the world, in hospital rooms and at deathbeds, with houseguests and strangers, and as a member of the mothers' prayer group at my children's school. And—coming full circle to my own childhood— every morning and every evening my husband and I gather before the throne with our three sons.

For the past nine years, I have also prayed at ten o'clock on Tuesday mornings with Carol, an older woman in my church. The two of us—sometimes joined by others—pray not only for the temporal and spiritual needs of our own church but especially for the concerns of the church throughout the world. On the last day, Carol and I will finally meet the redeemed from Peru and Thailand and Iran and Turkey and Sierra Leone, the brothers and sisters for whom we prayed.

These are my stories, but this book is a call to each one of us to consider the praying together we have done and are doing and hope to do: the childhood dinner-time prayers, the youth-group prayer vigils, the spontaneous prayer in dorm rooms and parking lots and at the back of the church, the planned prayer during Bible studies and prayer meetings and in the Lord's Day worship service. Here, too, you'll find reminders of our collective past. Adam's grandchildren and Daniel's friends and the apostles. The men on Fulton Street in 1858 whose prayer meeting set New York on fire. Those stories belong to all of us who belong to Christ. This book is a call to pray together and to keep praying together with renewed energy.

This book is not an exhaustive theology of prayer. Many and better minds than my own have written that book several times over. (As my husband gently reminded me when I first discussed this project with him, "But, Megan, *J. I. Packer* wrote a book on prayer."[3] When my girlfriend heard that, she added with a grin, "And you ain't no Packer, babe." So true. Which of us is?)

It's not an exhaustive theology, but it does contain theology. As Packer himself wrote, "True praying is an activity built on a theology."[4] You'll notice this book is divided into three parts. In the first part, The Foundations of Praying Together, we'll examine *why* we pray together. It might seem easier or more useful to jump straight to practical how-tos, but praying together is not an easy kind of task, and if we are not first constrained and encouraged by the testimony of Scripture, we will quickly give up. The second part, The Fruits of Praying Together, is a different kind of *why*. This section is a vision for what God says he does when we pray together and what he has done in the past when his people gathered together before his throne. Both are glorious motivations for the work. Finally, the third part, The Practice of Praying Together, explores *how*. Here, we'll consider what praying together can and does look like in our churches, communities, and homes. It is my own prayer that the people of Christ's church would again be like those saints of old who "devoted themselves to . . . the prayers" (Acts 2:42).

There is a vital work for us to do—for the love of Christ, for the exaltation of his name, for the glory of God. For the good of Christ's church for whom he died. For the good of our neighbors both local and global. For the good of our own souls.

This is a work for all of us. This great kingdom work that we have been given is open to all—to all who have been lost and found. Pastors and elders, yes, and the people in the pews too. We can start together this morning, or over lunch, or anytime tomorrow. This is work for those who travel the world and those who spend their days in a wheelchair. We can do this work anywhere. A church building is great, but that third-world street corner or this suburban living room will do just fine too.

There is work for all of us to do together. This is a work for mature believers—those for whom trends in Christianity are on their third or fourth replay—alongside the newly reborn. This is work for all those whose sins are big and whose Savior is bigger. It's for the academic and the mechanic and the mother of five. There is an important place in this work for the ill, the weak, the old, the tired. There is a place for the strong.

All who belong to Jesus, come and join us. You who are male and female, come. You adults and children, come. Invite the millennials—and the amillennials and premillennials too. Come, you who struggle to buy gas for your car, and you whose car uses no gas at all. Come, you who oversee charities and fund ministries, come sit beside this one whose mind and body are passing away but whose soul never will. Come together to this great privilege, this heavenly gathering, this means of grace, this vital task. Come.

Brothers and sisters, let us pray.

PART 1

THE FOUNDATIONS
OF PRAYING
TOGETHER

1

Relationship

A Christian never prays alone.

Thinking about prayer, we might first call to mind a picture of a lone man on his knees behind closed doors. We might think of him as solitary and his activity as private. But prayer is never solitary. It is communication from one to another. And so this book about praying together must begin with the foundational reality that *prayer is an activity of relationship*: God and us, God and God, all of us and our God.

God and Us

In 2012, when my husband and I walked through the gates of an orphanage in Addis Ababa, Ethiopia, we were immediately stampeded by twenty-five children. They grabbed at our backpacks, jabbed exploring fingers into our pockets, and repeatedly demanded our attention with the only English words they knew: "Mommy, Mommy, Mommy!" and "Daddy, Daddy, Daddy!"

Those little ones knew the language of family and the gestures of asking, but twenty-four of the children had no right to use them. And though we gave candy and balloons to every child, there was only one little boy whose cries to us of "Mommy" and

"Daddy" were absolutely compelling. This was the child with whom we had a relationship—having just appeared before a judge in a courtroom to secure his adoption—and this child alone could reach into our pockets with every assurance that he'd be granted whatever treat he could find there.

So, too, prayer is an activity of relationship. God placed the newly created Adam and Eve in the garden, and he spoke with them (Gen. 2:16–17; 3:2–3). Relationship is an essential part of our created nature (though now corrupted by sin), and communication is a crucial element of that relationship. In the introduction I defined prayer, in part, as "an offering up of our desires unto God."[1] Immediately, this tells us that prayer requires at least two participants: someone with desires and God. And Christ taught his disciples to pray "Our Father" (Matt. 6:9), establishing our prayers as the confident communication of a child with his parent.

Many people don't understand that prayer is intimately relational. Sociologist Christian Smith exhaustively studied the religious life of American teens and young adults and then famously described their attitude toward God as "moralistic therapeutic deism." By this Smith meant, in part, that "God is treated as something like a cosmic therapist or counselor, a ready and competent helper who responds in times of trouble but who does not particularly ask for devotion or obedience."[2]

An example of this kind of no-relationship-necessary perspective on prayer comes at the beginning of a recent best seller: Prayer is "communication from the heart to that which surpasses understanding. Let's say it is communication from one's heart to God. Or if that is too triggering or ludicrous a concept for you, to the Good, the force that is beyond our comprehension but that in our pain or supplication or relief we don't need to define or have proof of or any established contact with."[3]

And even 450 years ago, John Calvin lamented that people in his day were practically praying: "O Lord, I am in doubt whether thou willest to hear me, but because I am pressed by anxiety, I flee to thee, that, if I am worthy, thou mayest help me."[4]

In these ways of thinking, prayer can never be an activity of relationship because this kind of God is not particularly interested in relationship, and our prayers to him don't depend on it. Prayer becomes merely the submission of a list of desires and complaints with scant hope of personal engagement on the receiving end. Unloading my concerns might make me feel lighter, but it doesn't make me less lonely. I can pray, but God might not pay any attention.

For a Christian, prayer always expresses a relationship: with the Father, through the work of the Son, by the power of the Spirit. However, even those of us who understand the relational foundation of prayer rightly pause at the audacity of shrieking, "Daddy! Daddy!" and grabbing at God's backpack. Prayer is an activity of relationship, but it is not a relationship of equals. For one thing, God is the high and holy Creator, and man is the creature. The foundation of what we know about God and about mankind is this statement: "Then the LORD God formed the man of dust from the ground and breathed into his nostrils the breath of life, and the man became a living creature" (Gen. 2:7). Before Adam was a person, he was dirt. God, on the other hand, is the one who sits above the circle of the earth and the one is who is beyond comparison (Isa. 40:22, 25). It is not merely old-fashioned convention or literary metaphor that calls God "King" and "Lord" and "Judge" and "Ruler."

Therefore, we dust-people approach God—relate to God—only on his terms. Like Queen Esther, we must wait for the king to extend his royal scepter toward us. It's amazing that he does. In the garden, the Creator of the world condescended to his creation, and they had a conversation. But then sin entered the world, and since Adam's fall, mankind has been estranged by his own willful wickedness from the holy God, who "cannot look at wrong" (Hab. 1:13). The very words God uses to describe sinful people are anti-relational: enemies, strangers, aliens, separated. God may speak to us, but we dare not speak to him. Like Isaiah, we need a burning coal to purify our lips.

To know what effect our sin has on our right to pray, we must go to the cross. Here at Golgotha, the God-man shoulders the wrath of God in our place, and here we find a prayer that is the most horrific to ever be uttered. Here, our condemned Savior cries out, "My God, my God, why have you forsaken me?" (Mark 15:34). And there is no answer.

Forsaken by God, cut off from relationship to the Father, Jesus's prayer as the accursed sin bearer was met only with silence. Seminary professor Edmund Clowney used to tell his students, "You haven't heard the cry of the Son until you've heard the Father who didn't answer."[5] What do our prayers justly deserve? Silence. And yet the God who rejected the prayer of the wrath-bearing Son accepts our prayers because of him. In the glorious words of the book of Hebrews:

> Therefore, brothers, since we have confidence to enter the holy places by the blood of Jesus, by the new and living way that he opened for us through the curtain, that is, through his flesh, and since we have a great priest over the house of God, let us draw near with a true heart in full assurance of faith, with our hearts sprinkled clean from an evil conscience and our bodies washed with pure water. (Heb. 10:19–22)

The Bible repeatedly describes our entry into the Christian life in terms of relationship.[6] We who were once far off have been brought near to God (Eph. 2:13). The familial words used in Scripture—God the Father, Christ the elder brother—are indicators that a life of faith is a life of relationship. When we trust in Christ for our salvation, we begin a relationship with the triune God. By our adoption and our union with Christ, we become part of God's family, with all the privileges of children in their father's house. As J. Todd Billings explains, "We . . . enter into the playful, joyous world of *living as children of a gracious Father, as persons united to Christ and empowered by the Spirit.*[7] Cleansed from sin, covered in Christ's righteousness, and adopted by the Father, we who could never before presume to pray are welcomed into conversation with God.

But it would be only half the story to say that our new relationship with God through Christ simply *enables* us to pray. It is perfectly correct (and even necessary) to say that Christ's blood and righteousness secure our *right* to pray, but that legal term—*right*—doesn't begin to describe the emotional intensity of a believer's longing to pray. In truth, our new relationship with our God *compels* us to pray.

"People who know their God are before anything else people who pray,"[8] writes J. I. Packer. And the kind of knowing Packer has in view is nothing less than the intimate, mutual, self-revealing, other-embracing knowledge of relationship. A relationship with our God not only enables us to pray but presses us toward it. God opens his hands, reveals unimagined treats, and tells us to ask for them. For our part, delighted by our God, overwhelmed by his love, governed by his commands, and thankful for his condescension toward us, we overflow in prayer.

Like the lover in Song of Solomon, we can't stop talking about our beloved. What is praise but telling God who he is? What is thanksgiving but savoring aloud the things he has done? What is confession but lamenting to God that we have sinned against him and how far short we fall of being like him—he who is awesome in holiness? And what is supplication but requesting that God would do those things he most delights to do? What joy! We who know our God, we who belong to him just like children belong to a father, love to pray.

God and God

And when we pray, we approach not only a God who has a relationship with us but a God who has a relationship with himself.

Our relationship with the God who is three-in-one assures us that all three will involve themselves in our praying—making the prayers of a Christian part of a grand, heavenly conversation.

The doctrine of the Trinity is sometimes viewed askance, more mind-teaser than encouragement to a life of faith. But the fact that God is Father, Son, and Spirit is essential to our faith, as Michael Reeves explains:

> This God will simply not fit into the mold of any other. For the Trinity is not some inessential add-on to God, some optional software that can be plugged into him. At bottom, this God is different, for at bottom . . . he is the Father, loving and giving life to his Son in the fellowship of the Spirit. A God who is in himself love, who before all things could "never be anything but love." Having such a God happily changes everything.[9]

Relating to a Trinitarian God who himself is love changes everything about prayer too. Nowhere is this clearer in Scripture than in Romans 8:

> For all who are led by the Spirit of God are sons of God. For you did not receive the spirit of slavery to fall back into fear, but you have received the spirit of adoption as sons, by whom we cry, "Abba! Father!" . . . Likewise the Spirit helps us in our weakness. For we do not know what to pray for as we ought, but the Spirit himself intercedes for us with groanings too deep for words. And he who searches hearts knows what is the mind of the Spirit, because the Spirit intercedes for the saints according to the will of God. . . . Who shall bring any charge against God's elect? It is God who justifies. Who is to condemn? Christ Jesus is the one who died—more than that, who was raised—who is at the right hand of God, who indeed is interceding for us. (vv. 14–15, 26–27, 33–34)

In prayer, we approach a loving, listening Father, and we are helped by the intercession of the Son and the groaning of the

Spirit. I have never forgotten my pastor-father declaring: "When we pray, God talks to God."[10]

Romans 8 reveals the Father to be the one who hears our cry of "Abba!" His "hearing" is much more than merely taking in information. When the Father promises to hear prayer, it is an assurance of his loving inclination to receive our prayer as acceptable and to answer it in his kindness.

The Father's desire to hear the prayers of his children is so radical that he says, "Before they call I will answer; while they are yet speaking I will hear" (Isa. 65:24). By the time we clear our throats, the Father is already listening. This is especially evident in the words of Jesus to his disciples: "In that day you will ask in my name, and I do not say to you that I will ask the Father on your behalf; for the Father himself loves you, because you have loved me and have believed that I came from God" (John 16:26–27). Without denying his own intercessory prayers, Jesus's focus here is a bold assurance that redeemed people have no barriers to approaching the Father. We who belong to the eternal Son have every confidence that we, too, will receive the Father's listening love.[11]

For his part, the Son is our mediator and intercessor. The sinless life and death of Christ are the basis of our freedom from condemnation before a holy God and are the means by which we receive the spirit of adoption and the right to approach God in prayer (Rom. 8:1, 15, 31–34). It is for this reason that we conclude our prayers "in Jesus's name." People who pray are entirely dependent on the mediating work of Christ, who appears on our behalf, bears us on his shoulders, binds us on his breast, and allows us to be heard in his person.[12]

Furthermore, Romans 8 also talks of the risen Christ, "who indeed is interceding for us" (v. 34). Savor this explanation from James Montgomery Boice:

> What does intercession mean here? In this context it must refer
> to Jesus' prayers for his people, much like his great prayer

of John 17, in which he prays for and receives all possible benefits of his death for them for the living of their Christian lives. It means there is no need you can possibly have to which the Lord Jesus Christ is indifferent. It means that there is no problem to which he will turn a deaf ear or for which he will refuse to entreat his Father on your behalf.[13]

Brothers and sisters, Jesus is praying to the Father for you! Just as he prayed for Job in the midst of suffering (Job 16:20–21),[14] just as he prayed for Peter before Satan sifted him (Luke 22:31–32), and just as he prayed for all of his disciples—including us—before they became his witnesses in the world (John 17), he continues to pray for his beloved ones in heaven, adding our concerns to the divine conversation. And the thought that Jesus is praying for us is one of our greatest encouragements to faithfulness in prayer. Several times while he was on the earth, Jesus practically took his disciples by the hand and led them to the place of prayer (Luke 9:28; 11:1; 22:39–46). Sit here, he said. Pray while I pray, he said. And so he says to us too. Our Jesus is always praying. Sit here and pray alongside him.

And there is another divine participant in this conversation. The Spirit, who is teacher and comforter, is also prayer partner who "intercedes for us with groanings too deep for words" and "intercedes for the saints according to the will of God" (Rom. 8:26, 27).

The Spirit does three things related to our prayer. First, the Spirit unites us to Christ; this is how we gain the right to pray in the first place. In Romans 8, he is the "Spirit of adoption as sons,[15] by whom we cry 'Abba! Father!'" (v.15). Second, the Spirit prompts us to pray. The Spirit moves our hearts toward prayer by convicting us of our sin, stirring up our affections for God, and rightly ordering our desires by the means of his Word. Finally, the Spirit helps us when we pray by praying those things we ought to pray: "He who searches hearts knows what is the mind of the Spirit, because the Spirit intercedes for the saints according to the will of God" (Rom. 8:27).

When we pray, the Father, Son, and Holy Spirit reveal themselves to be the perfectly unified, triune God who is always of the same mind. It is correct to think of all God's answers to our prayers as either "Yes" or "Let me give you something better" [16] because of the intercession of the Spirit, who takes our prayers and molds them to match the will of God.

This knowledge that God talks to God motivates our praying in two remarkable ways. First, Trinitarian participation in prayer frees us from trusting in our prayers themselves. Prayer is not a magic incantation, dependent on us getting our abracadabras pronounced correctly, asking for exactly the right thing in exactly the right way at exactly the right time. The God who is love is not bound by faulty prayers, nor does he ignore the imperfect prayers of his beloved children. Instead, the one-in-three in whom we trust lovingly takes all our prayers, cleanses them of sin, and reorients them to match his holy will.

Secondly, when God talks to God, it encourages us to pray by assuring us that prayer is not merely happy thoughts (or desperate thoughts) tossed into a void. Our prayers are not pennies tossed into a fountain or wishes gone up in the smoke of birthday candles blown out. No. Prayer is the occasion of a divine conversation—a confident request for the loving persons of the Trinity to discuss and to act.[17] Listen to Reeves again: "And so the Spirit supports us, the Son brings us, and the Father—who always delights to hear the prayers of his Son—hears us with joy."[18]

Brothers and sisters, a Christian never—never!—prays alone.

All of Us and Our God

We pray as people who have a relationship with a God who has a relationship with himself. We also pray as people who, therefore, have a relationship with all the others who belong to him. Recently I heard a certain man described as "human Velcro." One of this man's greatest joys is to introduce his friends to each other and then encourage them to form a friendship together. This is exactly what our Lord does. Having first attached us firmly to himself by the bonds of his grace, he then introduces us to his other friends so that we might all stick together.

In order to embrace the practice of praying together, we first have to understand that Christians are, in fact, together. The church in Scripture is called a plant (John 15:1–17), a building (Eph. 2:18–22), and a body (Rom. 12:4–5; 1 Cor. 12:12–27; Eph. 4:15–16).[19] These three images emphasize our connectedness to one another through our essential relationship to Christ our Savior. In the plant image, Christ is the central vine and his people are the branches, dependent on him for nourishment and growth. In the building, we are the parts of the structure resting on the teaching of the apostles and prophets as our foundation and leaning into Christ as the cornerstone who holds us all together. Finally, in the image of the church as a body, we are diverse and interdependent parts that are "to grow up in every way into him [Christ] who is the head" (Eph. 4:15).

This necessary and organic interconnectedness in the church goes against the individualism of our day. One of Smith's other findings was that people think "each individual is uniquely distinct from all others and deserves a faith that fits his or her singular self . . . [and] that religion need not be practiced in and by a community."[20] Actually, believers can't opt out of community any more than a branch can separate itself from connection to other branches on the same tree. Our union to Christ necessarily joins us to everyone else who is united to him. Throughout the New Testament, the church is described as those who are "in Christ" (1 Cor. 1:2; Gal. 1:22; Eph. 1:1; Col. 1:2; 1 Thess. 2:14; 1 Pet. 5:14). And Jesus prayed for his disciples in all times and places "that they may all be one, just as you, Father, are in me, and I in you, that they also may be in us, so that the world may believe that you have sent me . . . I in them and you in me, that they may become perfectly one" (John 17:21, 23). Jesus sticks us all together.

Christ secures our relationship with other believers, and the

Spirit applies his guarantee, but we, too, must work on it. We ought to be "eager to maintain the unity of the Spirit in the bond of peace" (Eph. 4:3). Our unity is completely dependent on the Spirit, who dwells in us, and we also take steps to maintain that unity: we come together for public Lord's Day worship, we serve one another, we encourage and exhort one another. And one of our primary expressions of relationship with people who are in Christ is gathering together at God's throne in prayer.

In praying together, we nurture our relationship with other Christians, uniting our hearts even as we unite our voices (Acts 4:24), together exalting our common Savior and together bearing one another's burdens. Nineteenth-century churches often called their weekday prayer meeting "the social prayer meeting" or "the social meeting."[21] This is apt. The church is a society under Christ, and we are right to think of praying together as the highest and most blessed kind of social event.

At dinnertime when my children stare at their plates and point out that their green beans are touching their chicken, I remind them: "It's all going to end up in the same place." Our prayers are like that too. John's vision in Revelation pulls back the curtain of heaven: "Another angel came and stood at the altar with a golden censer, and he was given much incense to offer with *the prayers of all the saints* on the golden altar before the throne, and the smoke of the incense, with *the prayers of the saints*, rose before God from the hand of the angel" (Rev. 8:3–4). Our prayers are all going to end up in the same place. Every time we pray together, letting our prayers mingle with the prayers of other saints, we mirror the collection in heaven.

And praying together foreshadows our heavenly future when we will join that "great multitude that no one could number, from every nation, from all tribes and peoples and languages, standing before the throne and before the Lamb, clothed in white robes, with palm branches in their hands, and crying out with a loud voice, 'Salvation belongs to our God who sits on the throne, and to the Lamb!'" (Rev. 7:9–10). Jonathan Edwards called heaven "a world of love,"[22] because there we will perfectly love—and be loved by—our God and his saints forever. In heaven we will exist in glorious togetherness: together dressed in the righteousness of Christ and together praising him with one loud voice.

Praying is an activity of relationship. Calvin said prayer is "an intimate conversation of the pious with God";[23] it is also the intimate conversation of God with God and is a precious opportunity for the intimate conversation of the people who are bound together in relationship to him. By praying together, we nurture our relationship with our triune God and with his people—a relationship that will never end.

2

Duty

After our aging car finally died on the mechanic's lift, my husband and I purchased a new car with a manual transmission. It was cheaper than the automatic model, and, though I'd never been able to drive a standard, I assured my husband I would learn. Two years later, I still can't drive it. Over the months I made some half-hearted attempts on the local back roads, but the expense of time and energy, coupled with the ease of my automatic transmission minivan sitting ready in the driveway, lulled me into inertia. Why drive it? I don't really have to.

I have a friend who couldn't drive a stick-shift car, either. But fifteen minutes after stepping off a plane in Brazil, someone handed him the keys to one. This car was to be his sole transportation for the years of mission work he and his wife were just beginning. Without this car, he wouldn't be able to purchase food, go to the doctor, or accomplish ministry. So my friend got in and drove. And today, the rhythms of gear and clutch and brake—extremely awkward for me—are second nature to him.

Like driving a manual transmission, our commitment to corporate[1] prayer hinges on our sense of its importance. Praying together is—as we said in the last chapter—a glorious expression of our divine and human relationships, a precious privilege purchased for us by the blood of Christ, and an essential activity of the common Spirit in us. Most of us would acknowledge that it is a good idea. Nevertheless, we often fail to make it a priority of our lives simply because we aren't convinced it is necessary.

But far from being an optional activity—something to be learned and practiced when we have nothing more pressing going on—praying together is, as Martyn Lloyd-Jones said, "the very essence and life of the Church."[2] And it is only the Scriptures, the inspired Word of God and the Christian's rule for all of faith and life, which can rightly convince us of this.

In this chapter, we will allow the Word of God to compel us with its commands—its *imperatives*—to pray together. In the next chapter, we will allow the Word of God to excite us with its precious promises—its *incentives*—to gather for prayer. In these two ways, the weight of Scripture will impress upon us that Christians must pray together.

The Mark of God's People throughout Redemptive History

In September 1646, John Eliot, a colonist and minister in Roxbury, Massachusetts, first traveled with two other ministers to a settlement of Algonquin in order to preach the gospel. At a second evangelistic meeting there a month later, Eliot led in corporate prayer, praying in the Algonquin language "in proof that if they [the Algonquin] thus prayed God could understand them." The Spirit blessed Eliot's meetings, and hundreds trusted Christ over the course of his lifelong ministry. Those Christians came to be known in the Massachusetts Bay Colony as "Praying Indians," and their settlements were called "Praying Towns." The distinguishing mark of these converts was their resolution, in the words of one new believer, to "leave off Powowing, and pray to God." No longer would Christ's Algonquin children gather together for witchcraft and debauchery; instead, they would gather for prayer.[3]

Throughout redemptive history, praying together has marked

the spiritual liveliness of God's gathered people. Just as the evidence of Saul's awakened heart was prayer—"behold, he is praying" (Acts 9:11)—so, too, the consistent evidence of spiritual life among groups of Christians is that they pray together. In all ages and places, wherever we gather together, we are praying people.

The Beginning

We don't have to venture far into the new-created world before we find people praying together. As early as Genesis 4:26 we are told, "At that time people began to call upon the name of the LORD." This tiny half verse, an account of the true first great awakening, is rich in its significance:

> In these straits [of surrounding godlessness] an urgent appeal is made to God, and a spirit of boldness and union is infused into God's people, to counteract the lawless lust and pride of which the cities of Cain have become the centers. A more marked separation is effected between the followers of Abel's faith and the infidel apostasy. Men are constrained to assume more distinctly the religious profession, and devote themselves more decidedly to the service of God; avoiding worldly conformity, and giving themselves more earnestly to prayer as their only refuge.[4]

Pre-circumcision and pre-Sinai, just a few years after the first promise of a serpent-crushing Savior, the children of Seth were set apart from their godless Cainite neighbors by their practice of uniting to call on the name of the Lord. A visitor to that society would have recognized the godly by this mark: they prayed together. And they have been doing it ever since.

Israel

As God's redemptive narrative unfolds in the Scriptures, we read that he covenanted with the descendants of Jacob and established a relationship with them under his law. God declared to his people

Israel how they ought to live and worship before him. And a vital part of their God-defined corporate practice was praying together.

Though we often think of it as an intensely personal book, the Psalms is a collection of songs and prayers given to God's people for corporate worship. Can we pray the psalms as individuals? Certainly. But their primary intent was for use by a gathered people. Prayers like Psalm 90, with its first-person-plural language—"our dwelling place," "we are brought to an end," "teach us to number our days," "satisfy us," "establish the work of our hands"—were the familiar supplications of an Israelite congregation at prayer (vv. 1, 7, 12, 14, 17).

When Solomon dedicated the temple, he actually prayed about praying. In the hearing of God's people, he asked God to receive both private and corporate prayer: "Whatever prayer, whatever plea is made by any man or by all your people Israel . . . then hear from heaven your dwelling place" (2 Chron. 6:29–30). The temple was a glorious place indeed! All Israel gathered for prayer, and God listened to them.

And it gets even better. Isaiah, as the prophetic mouthpiece of God, expanded Solomon's vision by declaring: "My house shall be called a house of prayer for all peoples" (Isa. 56:7). The promised future of God's people included all nations and peoples gathered together in prayer. As one commentator explains, "Here is the beauty of holiness; men from all nations, brought to His household by sovereign grace, lift up the sacrifice of prayer unto His holy name, which they love, and in His Name serve Him in His house."[5] The Old Testament strained toward that day when God's diverse people in diverse places would be united together in prayer.

Exile

But before the nations would come among God's people, his people would be scattered among the nations. Their persistent rebellion against the one true God and treacherous love for other gods resulted in their just judgment and exile. Dispersed and relocated,

God's people in exile lived a life of faith without the outward markers of a physical temple or priestly worship. Even while they lived among pagans, corporate prayer distinguished God's people as holy.

Daniel was a young Israelite man taken to Babylon to serve in the court of Nebuchadnezzar. He and his three friends were separated from their families, given new names, trained in pagan culture, and counted among the magicians and sorcerers in the king's court. But early in their story Scripture assures us that they were not captive to the godlessness around them. Faced with the threat of death, and asked to interpret a dream he hasn't heard, Daniel is markedly different from the hand-wringing, prevaricating wise men. Daniel and his friends prayed together: "Then Daniel went to his house and made the matter known to Hananiah, Mishael, and Azariah, his companions, and told them to seek mercy from the God of heaven concerning this mystery, so that Daniel and his companions might not be destroyed with the rest of the wise men of Babylon" (Dan. 2:17–18).

After God answered their prayer and revealed the dream, the group went into action. There was urgent business at hand. The impatient and capricious king was waiting. The life of every wise man in the country was at stake. The reputation of the God of Israel was on trial. And Daniel and his friends chose the most urgent activity first: they praised God in prayer together (Dan. 2:20–23).

Esther, too, contrasted sharply with the wickedness around her. Like Daniel—taken from her family, immersed in the life of pagan royalty, and placed under the threat of death—Esther called for a prayer meeting: "Then Esther told them to reply to Mordecai, 'Go, gather all the Jews to be found in Susa, and hold a fast on my behalf, and do not eat or drink for three days, night or day. I and my young women will also fast as you do'" (Est. 4:15–16). Prayer always accompanies fasting in the Scripture, and Esther was undoubtedly calling people to pray.[6]

These two young people didn't have parents or priests to tell them to pray together. Their knowledge of God's ways and their true faith in him drew them to it. Even when God's people are strangers in a strange land and hard-pressed on every side, they gather together for prayer.

Return

As the prophets had foretold, many of God's people did return to the land from their exile. They again established families and towns, worked with their hands, and worshiped in the newly rebuilt temple. And they prayed together.

When Ezra set out with a group of returning exiles, he immediately initiated a fast: "Then I proclaimed a fast there, at the river Ahava, that we might humble ourselves before our God, to seek from him a safe journey for ourselves, our children, and all our goods. . . . So we fasted and implored our God for this, and he listened to our entreaty" (Ezra 8:21, 23). As the leader, Ezra knew his responsibility to call people to pray together.

After they arrived in the land, it became known that the covenant people had sinfully intermarried with the pagans there. In the face of this news, the people themselves were moved to pray together. The Bible doesn't mention any general call from Ezra, but "a very great assembly of men, women, and children" gathered alongside him in repentance and lament (Ezra 10:1). Confronted with their sin, the hearts of "all who trembled at the words of the God of Israel" moved them to come together and pray (Ezra 9:4).

Jesus

In the fullness of time, the redemptive narrative brings us to its climax: Jesus. We pray "in Jesus's name" because he is the one whose blood secures our right to pray, whose perfect will and blameless character direct our prayers, and whose ongoing intercession in heaven makes us bold on our knees. This Jesus is also our highest example and best teacher in the school of praying together.

In the previous chapter, we talked about Jesus's habit of leading his disciples together to the place of prayer. Those men were familiar with the practice of praying together, and when they asked Jesus to teach them to pray, he responded by giving them corporate language to use: "Our Father. . . . Give us this day our daily bread . . . forgive us our debts . . . as we also have forgiven our debtors. . . . Lead us not into temptation, but deliver us from evil" (Matt. 6:9–13). Jesus taught his disciples not only to pray in private (Matt. 6:6) but also to pray with and for others, praying to their common Father for their common needs.[7]

Later, when Jesus cleansed the temple, he jealously guarded corporate prayer as a priority for God's people, repreaching Isaiah's designation "house of prayer" (Matt. 21:13; Mark 11:17; Luke 19:46; cf. Isa. 56:7). Perhaps surprisingly to his hearers, Jesus did not define the place of worship as a place of sacrifice.[8] Instead, for those distracted by the hustle of pigeon salesmen and white-collar criminals, Jesus focused on what God's people should do when they gathered. He told them to pray together.

Heaven

We will not be permanently and fully gathered until we are gathered in heaven. And there, too, Jesus will bid his disciples to pray. He is the "voice from the throne" commanding the multitude: "Praise our God, all you his servants" (Rev. 19:5).[9] And he is our elder brother, leading the congregation in praise (Heb. 2:12).

If we consider prayer to be asking God for something we don't have, it might be strange to think about praying together as perfected people in the new creation. But if we remember that prayer is "an offering up of our desires unto God . . . with thanksgiving,"[10] we see that praying together will be important in heaven too. Some of the elements of our prayer on earth will be unnecessary in heaven, of course. Our sins will be vanished—and along with them our practice of confession. Our needs will be fully met—our days illuminated by the Lamb himself, our bellies filled by his wedding feast, and our tears wiped by his nail-pierced hands—and we will not have to ask for daily bread. But what remains will be prayer nonetheless, our united offering of one pure desire: the eternal glory of our God. We will join our voice to the multitude of saints and forever pray, "Hallelujah! . . . Let us rejoice and exult and give him the glory" (Rev. 19:5–7).

But what does heaven have to do with us? G. K. Beale explains it this way:

> Christians are like pilgrims passing through this world. As such they are to commit themselves to the revelation of God in the new order so as progressively to reflect and imitate his image and *increasingly live according to the values of the new world*, not being conformed to the fallen system, its idolatrous images, and associated values.[11]

As citizens of heaven, we Christians live according to the priorities of a better country. And if praying together is an important work of heaven, then it also ought to be important to God's people on earth. Frequently, the writers of the New Testament tie faithfulness in prayer to our expectation of heaven. First Thessalonians 5:12–24; Philippians 4:5–6; and Jude 20–21 all compel Christians to pray in light of the imminent approach of Christ. Also, Hebrews 10:24–25 encourages us to meet together "all the more as you see the Day drawing near." God's Word uses the prospect of eternal worship together to inspire us to pursue those things with greater fervency now.

Acts: Our Foundation

Surrounded by this great cloud of witnesses—God's people in all ages and places whose lives are a testimony and encouragement to pray together—we come to the book of Acts. Acts not only stands in line with the previous eras of redemptive history, but it also provides the foundation for the church until the end of the age.

In Acts we find the clearest picture of the priorities of the New Testament church: we follow the path of the gospel from Jerusalem to the ends of the earth and watch its effects wherever it went. In its twenty-eight chapters, occasions of praying together are mentioned explicitly twenty times and implicitly many more.[12] We read that Christians in Acts prayed together regularly, concertedly, and intentionally. But those early Christians did not invent praying together. Their corporate prayer was connected to the prayer during the previous thousands of years of covenant history. The early Christians knew the cloud of witnesses too.

The practice of the Christians in Acts also carefully lays the foundation for the next stage in redemptive history—from Christ's ascension until his return—reaching forward and defining the shape of the church into our present time. As Dennis Johnson explains, "The foundational, apostolic period may have some unique features about it, just because it is foundational, but the foundation also determines the contours of the building to be constructed on it."[13] These believers in Acts prayed together because God's people have always been—must always be!—praying people.

We are first introduced to them while they are waiting for the promised Spirit: "All these with one accord were devoting themselves to prayer, together with the women and Mary the mother of Jesus, and his brothers" (Acts 1:14). This verse highlights the characteristics of corporate prayer which repeat throughout Acts. Their prayer was deliberate ("devoted"), it was united ("with one accord"), and it included the full diversity of Christians ("all these . . . with the women . . . and his brothers").

From this verse onward, Luke records the church's foundational priority of corporate prayer. Christians in Acts prayed together:

- at the selection of Judas's replacement (1:24);
- after Pentecost, as a mark of the spiritual life of the new believers (2:42);
- at shared meals (2:46);
- at the set times in the temple (3:1);

- for boldness, when faced with the threat of persecution (4:23–31);
- as the special priority of the apostles (6:4);
- for the Spirit, with the church at Samaria (8:15–17);
- in the middle of the night for Peter when he was imprisoned (12:5, 12);
- at the sending of Barnabas and Saul (13:1–3);
- when appointing elders for the church and committing them to the Lord (14:23);
- at the sending of Paul and Silas through Syria and Cilicia (15:40);
- on the Sabbath with the devout women of Philippi (16:13);
- at the place of prayer in Philippi again (16:16);
- in the prison in Philippi at midnight (16:25);
- with the Ephesian elders as Paul departs for Jerusalem (20:36–38);
- in Tyre with the disciples and their wives and children; for Paul as he sets sail for Jerusalem (21:5–6);
- with thanksgiving for food onboard the ship (27:35–38);
- for Publius's father on the island of Malta (28:8);
- with the brothers in Rome who traveled to meet Paul (28:15).

For the early church, there was much to do. But essential to their gospel-proclaiming, bread-breaking, widow-feeding, and church-planting work was praying together. These early Christians—diverse, united, and devoted—prayed together when they arrived and when they departed. They prayed together when they were sick and imprisoned but also when they were simply sitting down for a meal. They prayed in the formal worship services of the temple and at the riverside prayer meetings. The apostles prayed together. Men and women and children prayed together. They prayed for the Spirit, for protection, for boldness in the proclamation of the gospel. They prayed for one another. Wherever the gospel went, wherever churches were established, God's people were praying people.

Brothers and sisters, can we think that Christians today ought to be any different?

Commands: Everybody, Everywhere, about Everything

And so we come at last to the direct commands—the explicit imperatives—of the New Testament Epistles. Again and again these Scriptures tell us to pray together.[14] With everybody. Everywhere. About everything.

The New Testament call to prayer includes everybody, together. In our individualistic culture we might be accustomed to receiving the apostle Paul's familiar "be constant in prayer" (Rom. 12:12) and "continue steadfastly in prayer" (Col. 4:2) as directives for private devotions. But these commands are not simply imperatives to personal prayer (though they certainly are that); they are imperatives to the church. The majority of the Epistles were letters to the church as a whole, to be read out in the assembly for worship (Col. 4:16; 1 Thess. 5:27), and their commands are firstly understood as being given to the corporate people of God.

"Brothers, pray for us" (1 Thess. 5:25, cf. 2 Thess. 3:1), writes Paul to the Thessalonians. Who are the brothers? Earlier in the letter, Paul calls them "the church" and those who are "loved by God" (1 Thess. 1:1, 4). This command to pray was received by the whole church together. Elsewhere, Paul asks for the prayers of a multitude: "You also must help us by prayer, so that many will give thanks on our behalf for the blessing granted us through the prayers of many" (2 Cor. 1:11). The church is not merely a roster of individuals who pray privately; it is a congregation that ought to pray together.

And what diverse congregations the New Testament churches were! The first hearers of the Epistles included men, women, children, slaves, Jews, Gentiles, rich people, poor people, and members of the royal household, orphans, widows, and people with disabilities, new converts, mature believers, and Christians who had been hoodwinked by false teachers. Today, too, we find ourselves worshiping alongside people of all ages, both genders, and a variety of abilities and gifts. The diverse people that make up the church are commanded to unite their voices in prayer. Just as the disciples and the women and the brothers prayed together "with one accord" (Acts 1:14) in the earliest moments of Christianity, and just as the Tyrian disciples and women and children prayed on the beach for Paul as he set off for Jerusalem (Acts 21:6–5), so, too, Christian disciples and women and children in the modern church should pray together.

The New Testament writers tell the church to pray, and these commands are of one piece with the rest of God's inerrant, authoritative, and inspired Word. Together with the Old Testament, the New Testament commands show us the way of godliness today. They speak with thundering consummation of Isaiah's prophesied "house of prayer for all people" (Isa. 56:7). They call to mind the great prayer meeting of Ezra's day, when men and women and children spontaneously gathered in corporate confession. And they echo the proclamation from the heavenly throne: "Praise our God, all you his servants, you who fear him, small and great" (Rev. 19:5).

The New Testament mandates for prayer include a diversity of people, but they also involve a diversity of situations. First, praying together ought to be a significant part of our public worship on the Lord's Day. Paul gives instructions for corporate worship, such as these: "I desire then that in every place the men should pray, lifting holy hands without anger or quarreling," and, "Is it proper for a wife to pray to God with her head uncovered?" (1 Tim. 2:8; 1 Cor. 11:13). The contemporary application of hand raising and head covering is much debated, but no one disputes that, fundamentally, these texts point to the necessity of prayer in corporate worship. Our prayer together in Lord's Day worship is simply an expression of what we find throughout the Scriptures. It echoes the corporate prayers of the psalms offered in the temple, it fulfills Jesus's instructions for our priority in public worship, and it extends the practice of the apostles, who continued to visit the temple and synagogues "at the hour of prayer" (e.g., Acts 3:1).

But, second, the duty to pray together continues throughout our week. We are not merely commanded to pray with the assembled saints on Sundays, checking it off a list of weekly duties. No, the command goes out for God's people to pray together "at all times" and "without ceasing" (Eph. 6:18; 1 Thess. 5:17). Like the covenant people in all ages, we ought to find ourselves praying together deliberately and fervently whenever we can. If the returning exiles paused at the riverside before beginning their journey, if Daniel and Esther called prayer meetings before addressing the king, if Paul and his companions prayed together in prisons and on beaches, in sick rooms and onboard ships, then we should do likewise. If the Christians in Acts were found praying for Paul at midnight, and if Paul, Silvanus, and Timothy declared themselves to be praying for the church "night and day" (1 Thess. 3:10), we must not be limited by normal business hours. When we pray together here, there, and everywhere on different days of the week and at various times of day and night—when we pray together "without ceasing"—we continue the perennial practice of God's people and fulfill the Lord's mandate.

By its commitment to praying together at all times, the church stands in stark contrast to the godlessness around her. Jude writes, "But you, beloved, building yourselves up in your most holy faith and praying in the Holy Spirit . . ." (Jude 20). Jude implores the church to pray in a manner that marks them as different from the surrounding godlessness. Christians today ought to be like the Sethites (Gen. 4:26) and like Daniel's friends and like Esther's maids, turning together toward God in a culture of great wickedness.

Finally, the New Testament Epistles command us to pray together about everything. We should pray together about everything as an antidote to anxiety (Phil. 4:5–6). We should pray together when one of us is sick or suffering or caught in sin (James 5:13–16). We should pray together for all Christians (Eph. 6:18), imploring God that his people could live in peace (1 Tim. 2:1–2). And we should pray for kingdom laborers, that they would live godly lives, be protected from persecution, and preach with the power of the Spirit (Heb. 13:18–19; 1 Thess. 5:25; 2 Thess. 3:1).

In the next chapters we will examine in greater detail the content of our prayers. But the fundamental instruction of the Epistles is that we are to pray together for all kinds of things. Just as the Psalms petition God for the whole range of human needs, just as Solomon encouraged "whatever plea" from the assembled Israelites (1 Kings 8:38), just as the church in Acts prayed for strong leaders for Christ's church and boldness to proclaim the gospel and open prison doors (Acts 1:24; 4:23–31; 12:5), so, too, we ought to present all of our requests to God.

Praying together should be a way of life for Christians. We should continue to bow our heads in public worship and at the family dinner table, and we should seek new opportunities to unite with others at God's throne. The Scriptures make it plain that our interactions with a variety of other Christians ought to overflow in prayer together as the ordinary practice of our life.

Brothers and sisters, we must be praying people.

3

Promise

God gives us promises. Having first commanded us to pray together, he then pledges to do us good when we obey. God says that when we pray together, he will defeat his enemies, proclaim his glory, revive our hearts, grant our requests, give us his presence, and bring healing. Under the loving affirmation of these words, we come together in prayer, knowing that our God will do great things.

Praying by Number?

We will focus on a few verses individually and savor their sweetness in a moment, but, first, let's try to understand the big picture. Sadly, people often interpret God's promises about praying together as a magic formula for getting a blessing. Martyn Lloyd-Jones wrote about a "mathematical notion of prayer" in which people wrongly believe certain circumstances surrounding prayer (length of time, number of repetitions, or effort of the person praying) will make their prayers more likely to secure God's blessing.[1] And we can make the same error when we read God's promises for praying together and believe that if we can just get enough people to ask God for something with enough boldness, he'll have to give it to us.

This leads us to have a diminished view of the Father's love for us. When we think God will not hear us or grant our requests unless we have a requisite number of people with a requisite amount of faith—piling enough friends on our end of the seesaw or collecting enough signatures on our petition—prayer together becomes an attempt to manipulate a grudging God. Nothing could be further from the true character of the Father, who repeatedly declares himself to be full of compassion and mercy, the giver of all good gifts, attentive to the cry of the weak and the forgotten, and eager to grant what his children ask.

Out of this generous love, he has given us his Son, who ever lives to intercede. Again and again in Scripture God shows his inclination to hear the prayers of even one person. Abraham alone pleaded for Sodom (Gen. 18:22–33). Moses alone interceded for Israel (Num. 14:13–19). Elijah was one godly man—things had gotten so bad in Israel that he thought he was the *only* godly man—whose prayer for rain was heard and granted by our Lord (James 5:17–18). And the sick man at Bethesda had no one to carry him to the pool, yet our Lord healed him where he lay, alone, at the water's edge (John 5:1–9). Why would the God of the universe hear the supplications of just one person? Because, as we noted in chapter 1, one person in prayer is never just one person. One person always has the indispensable help of the Three: the Son, whose blood secures our right to pray; the Father, who always hears those who belong to him; and the Spirit, who knows the mind of God and helps us accordingly. No configuration of people praying together—not two people or two million people, not a company of especially holy people or of especially fervent people—can ever make our prayers more acceptable or more compelling to the Father. Christ alone is our mediator. His perfect work—and only his work!—guarantees that our prayers receive a loving welcome before the Father.

The church father Tertullian rightly understood God's promises when he described praying together as "a holy conspiracy [by which] we may set upon God by a force that is welcome to him."[2] The terms of our conspiracy are holy: they are established by the Lord and practiced at his direction. Our conspiracy is also welcome: it is attended by Christ's intercession and encouraged by his promises. We "set upon God" only because he has first thrown open the door to blessing and invited us in. Through his gracious promises, our loving Father declares what he intends to give and presents us with glorious incentive to ask him for it together.

Let's look now at five Scripture passages that show how God uses our united prayer.

Warfare and Judgment

Another angel came and stood at the altar with a golden censer, and he was given much incense to offer with the prayers of all the saints on the golden altar before the throne. . . . Then the angel took the censer and filled it with fire from the altar and threw it on the earth, and there were peals of thunder, rumblings, flashes of lightning, and an earthquake. (Rev. 8:3, 5)

Praying together is a tactical maneuver in God's great war against Satan and his kingdom. Ephesians 6 concludes its description of our spiritual armor against evil with an imperative to take up the offensive tactic of prayer (Eph. 6:18). As John Calvin commented, "We ought to fight by our prayers and supplications."[3] In the hands of one believer, prayer is a single weapon against a mighty enemy. In the hands of gathered people, prayer is an arsenal for the army of the Lord, enabling us to "withstand in the evil day" (Eph. 6:13). By the prayers of many, God's people are led away from temptation and delivered from evil (Matt. 6:13). By prayer together, Satan's subjects wave the white flag of surrender, and his demons are defeated (Mark 9:29). By prayer together, the gospel of Jesus Christ secures victory in people's hearts (2 Thess. 3:1). Even the united praises of little children force Satan to shut his mouth (Ps. 8:2). The Evil One may roar at the church, but the church at prayer attacks the gates of hell. And the gates of hell will crumble (Matt. 16:18).

Our praying together will culminate in the last day, in the final hour of judgment for the wicked and rebellious. In John's vision in Revelation, the seventh seal is opened, and the combined prayers of the saints ascend from the hand of an angel before the great throne. God answers these prayers by sending judgment: [4] "Then the angel took the censer and . . . threw it on the earth, and there were peals of thunder, rumblings, flashes of lightning, and an earthquake" (Rev. 8:5). The prayers of the saints are used by God to bring judgment on his enemies. Our prayers are a spiritual force, and many—perhaps *most*—of the answers to our prayers happen in the unseen places. Our struggle is not against flesh and blood but is a war against the forces of evil (Eph. 6:12), and praying saints are God's chosen army for the defeat of his dying enemy.

Brothers and sisters, "the prayers of the saints and the fire of God move the whole course of the world." [5]

Glory and Honor

> All your works shall give thanks to you, O LORD,
>   and all your saints shall bless you!
> They shall speak of the glory of your kingdom
>   and tell of your power,
> to make known to the children of man your mighty deeds,
>   and the glorious splendor of your kingdom.
>   (Ps. 145:10–12)

When my husband and I drive through the streets of a new city at mealtime, we keep our eyes open for a place to eat. A restaurant doesn't have to be big, or famous, or fancy. Instead, we look for a full parking lot. Fifteen cars in front of a tiny building means that—no matter how flaky the paint or greasy the windows—this is a place worth stopping. The presence of the other diners convinces us to entrust our appetites to whoever is standing in that kitchen, and we are rarely disappointed. Likewise, when God's people gather for prayer, it's a testimony to the world's passersby: Look over here! We found something good!

Repeatedly in Scripture, God takes pleasure in the praise and worship of many. "Oh, magnify the LORD with me," invites David in another psalm, "and let us exalt his name together!" (Ps. 34:3). Our God is not a God who delights to hide himself but one who delights to make himself known everywhere, and especially among his people. His answers to our requests and his kindnesses toward us become an opportunity for the many to give thanks (2 Cor. 1:11), and our prayer together is a preview of that day when "every knee shall bow" and "every tongue shall confess" (Rom. 14:11).

When we pray together, we declare in the hearing of others who our God is—we build an arena in which to showcase God's sovereign work and his gracious character. Our corporate prayers demonstrate that we are a people who know our God and who delight in his ways: "He is your praise" (Deut. 10:21). And God uses our words of praise and thanksgiving to make himself and his kingdom known "to the children of man" (Ps. 145:12). By our united praises, says Matthew Henry, we invite all people "to yield themselves his willing subjects and so put themselves under the protection of such a mighty potentate."[6] When we pray together, God glorifies himself among all who hear.

Forgiveness and Revival

> When I shut up the heavens so that there is no rain, or command the locust to devour the land, or send pestilence among my people, if my people who are called by my name humble themselves, and pray and seek my face and turn from their wicked ways, then I will hear from heaven and will forgive their sin and heal their land. (2 Chron. 7:13–14)

With his words to Solomon, the Lord tells us that we ought to have an attitude of humility as we pray together. In the act of praying together—asking God for what we cannot do for ourselves—we publicly acknowledge the difference between him and us, and we admit our dependence on him. We confess our sin, rebuking Satan and declaring our allegiance to God. And we also unite our voices to seek God's face. As Jonathan Edwards explained, in seeking God's face we are seeking God himself:

> But certainly that expression of "seeking the Lord," is very commonly used to signify something more than merely, in general, to seek some mercy of God: it implies, that God himself is the great good desired and sought after; that the blessings pursued are God's gracious presence, the blessed manifestations of him, union and intercourse with him; or, in short, God's manifestations and communications of himself by his Holy Spirit.[7]

The chief request of God's people is for the Holy Spirit (cf. Luke 11:11–13). And in answer to our supplication, God promises to pour out his grace: "Then I will hear from heaven and will forgive their sin and heal their land." In response to our humility, the Father condescends to hear us. In response to our confession, he exalts his Son by forgiving our sins. In response to our desire to know him, he lavishes his people with his Spirit.

Brothers and sisters, when we pray together, God sends revival.

We will look more closely at revival in chapter 6; for now, we can simply delight in the fact that these verses promise it.[8] In answer to the united, humble prayers of his people, God pledges to stir and refresh the hearts of his children and to pour out his Spirit upon his church. Like rain after a drought, a harvest after the locusts, and healing after an illness, God revives his people when they pray together.

Agreement and Fellowship

Again I say to you, if two of you agree on earth about anything they ask, it will be done for them by my Father in heaven. For where two or three are gathered in my name, there am I among them. (Matt. 18:19–20)

Jesus's promise here appears in the primary context of church discipline, but we can also make a secondary application to prayer.[9] In Matthew 18 Christ promises to be with us, and the Father promises to answer us when we pray together. The glorious theme of this passage is agreement: the assembled believers agree with Christ ("for where two or three are gathered in my name, there am I among them"); the believers agree with one another ("if two of you agree"); and the Father agrees with their united prayer ("it will be done for them by my Father in heaven"). Like strands of a rope, these three threads of agreement are inseparable.

When I was in college, I joined the synchronized swimming team. I loved to swim and thought the sport might be a fun, new experience. Over the months of practice, I learned to keep myself afloat with just my hands, to dive without a ripple from the surface of the water, and to turn in graceful spirals while upside-down underwater. But the skills themselves were not the most difficult part. The greatest challenge was synchronizing myself with my teammates. Sometimes we would have nearly thirty women in the pool, all attempting to do the same thing at the same time. If we oriented ourselves to what we each thought the others were doing, our timing lagged and our formations were skewed. Measuring our movements against other moving people always made practices a disaster, and the coach became understandably frustrated. But if we all paid attention to fixed markers outside of us—the beats of the music and our place in the pool—we ended up perfectly aligned and received the applause of our coach.

So, too, when we pray together, we can only be agreed when we orient our desires toward something outside ourselves. The unmoved and unmoving reference point for our gathered prayers is not a physical location (Christians have neither Mecca nor temple) but a person. We unite in Jesus's name—through his merit, at his bidding, under his authority—and with the assurance of his presence. Abiding in him and meditating on his Word (John 15:7), we bring our hearts into agreement with Christ. Like swimmers in a pool, aligning our requests to Christ causes us to agree with one another and allows our united prayer to receive the Father's affirmation.

Tertullian called praying together "a holy conspiracy,"[10] and so it is. With humility and thanksgiving, we conspire together with one another and with Christ to approach the Father. Even the tiniest group has Christ's promise of fellowship: "Where two or three are gathered in my name, there am I among them" (Matt. 18:20). We gather in his name, with his brothers, proclaiming his praises, and asking for things that please him. Then, by his Spirit, he will be there too. When a handful of people pray together, Jesus will attend every time. And the Father will not deny the requests of a prayer meeting where Christ is also praying.

Our prayer meetings have the power of Christ's presence and of his intercession so that anything that pleases Christ, anything that fulfills his purpose, anything that glorifies him, anything he commands or promises or loves, we ask with one voice together with Christ in confident expectation that the Father will answer.

Brothers and sisters, how could we stay away?

Healing and Salvation

> Is anyone among you sick? Let him call for the elders of the church, and let them pray over him, anointing him with oil in the name of the Lord. And the prayer of faith will save the one who is sick, and the Lord will raise him up. And if he has committed sins, he will be forgiven. (James 5:14–15)

In this promise, James gives direction for the church member who is seriously ill, commanding the elders of the church to pray together and commending "the prayer of faith" (v. 15). These verses specifically exhort elders to the work of prayer, an essential priority of church leaders from the apostles on.

This promise also has a broader application, and James quickly follows it with a general exhortation to pray for "one another" (v. 16). If Mary and Martha sent together for the Lord when Lazarus became ill (John 11:1–44), certainly we, too, should stand together beside hospital beds and call on Jesus. If our Lord healed the paralytic because of the faith of his friends (Matt. 9:1–7), we, too, can lay our suffering brothers and sisters at his feet through the prayer of faith.

But what do we place our faith in? When my dad was diagnosed with leukemia, his non-Christian oncologist told him, "With this chemotherapy treatment, 90 percent of patients go into remission. I'm confident it will be a good option for you." This doctor had lots of faith—in a drug, in the research studies, and in his own judgment. Similarly, gathered around the bedside of a sick person, groups of some professing Christians may declare their conviction that healing will certainly happen and demand in prayer that God do it. As one best-selling author asserted, "I am confident that you are only one prayer away from a dream fulfilled, a promise kept, or a miracle performed."[11] Though this expectation might sound good, such people demonstrate misplaced faith too—in the power of prayer to bring about the result they want. These examples are not the kind of faith James is talking about.

That's because the Christian's faith is never placed in circumstances. While non-Christians might have faith in medical techniques, and professing Christians might have faith in their own boldness, the true "prayer of faith" expresses faith in a person. It is faith in the triune God, the Creator of heaven and earth and the architect of our salvation. It is faith in the almighty God who placed the stars, dresses the lilies, catches fallen sparrows, and knows each hair on our head (Ps. 8:2; Matt. 6:28–29; 10:29–31). It is faith in the God who has so often been pleased to glorify himself and do good to his people by forgiving their sins, defeating their enemies, healing their illnesses, providing for their needs, and giving them cause for rejoicing (Ps. 103:2–5). It is faith in the God who is "able to do far more abundantly than all that we ask" (Eph. 3:20).

Moreover, as Douglas Moo notes, the prayer of faith "also involves absolute confidence in the perfection of God's will."[12] Not only do we pray believing in a God who *can* do anything; we pray believing in a God who *will* do—*always* does!—what is best. The prayer of faith never demands from God but instead bows before God, who works all things for the good of those who love him (Rom. 8:28). It is faith in the God to whom we have never given anything and yet who gives to us every good and perfect gift (Rom. 11:35; James 1:17). It is faith in the God who, if necessary, also gives us trials and suffering (1 Pet. 1:6–7; James 1:2–3). It is faith in the Father who did not spare his own Son and therefore does not begrudge us anything else that is best for us (Rom. 8:23; Ps. 84:11). And it is faith in the God who, as we saw in chapter 1, always answers our prayers with either "Yes" or "Let me give you something better."

In James 5, then, the Lord promises both temporal and spiritual answers when we pray together in faith: "The prayer of faith will save the one who is sick, and the Lord will raise him up. And if he has committed sins, he will be forgiven" (v. 15). In many cases, God's gracious answer to the elders' prayer will be physical healing. The sick child of God will take up her mat and walk. Certainly our Lord is able to heal physical infirmities of all kinds; when he was on the earth Jesus gave sight to the blind, speech to the mute, and hearing to the deaf. His power is so great that he even cured ten men in a single instant (Luke 17:11–14). Let no one think that any illness might be beyond the reach of the God who knit our bodies together in the secret place. If physical healing is best, he will use our prayers to do it.

The Lord also promises spiritual answers to our prayers. The language that James uses for God's answer—"save" and "raise"—

has both physical and spiritual meaning.[13] Often in prayer, we tend one way or another. Some Christians pray a hospital roll call. Other Christians request only spiritual good. James encourages both. We can pray together for physical healing and for spiritual renewal, for freedom from disease and for forgiveness of sins, for whole bodies and for rebirthed souls. By our prayer together, God brings many people who have been laid low by illness to repentance and faith. And he promises that his suffering children will be raised to glorious resurrection bodies at the last day (1 Cor. 15:51–54). As Daniel Doriani notes, "The Lord will heal all his people sooner or later."[14]

Because of this encouragement, we are not afraid that our prayers might be too big or suspicious that our big prayers might receive the wrong answer. We have absolute confidence in a God who promises to use our united prayer of faith to do the very best thing.

Socks and Oranges

We've just seen five glorious promises from our gracious Lord. But if our hearts are far from God, we might receive these promises like the boy who thinks he's going to get candy but wakes up Christmas morning to socks and oranges. Socks and oranges are actually amazing gifts: protection and nourishment! Warmth and sweetness! They are much more substantial than even the biggest box of chocolates, but they still appear dull to a kid who anticipated something else.

So, too, the promises of God for praying together—spiritual victory, God's glory, revival, fellowship, salvation—could seem dull to someone who expected a lollipop. These big and weighty promises only appeal to those whose priorities and values have been conformed to Christ. And it's the humble child, the one who aligns his heart with the desires of his parents, the one who trusts them to give what is best, who can squeal with delight as he opens his gifts. Our Father is the loving parent who will not promise us candy when socks and oranges are far better. The goal for us, then, is to learn to love them because God does. It's to joyfully wiggle our warm toes, drops of bright juice on our lips, and to recognize in God's promises more than all we could ask or think.

Slightly Imperfect

Considering these promises, we also might find ourselves despairing at our failures in corporate prayer. Recently I was scrolling the website of a popular Christian bookseller, when I noticed a shopworn volume advertised on clearance as *At the Throne of Grace: A Book of Prayers—Slightly Imperfect.* I laughed because I could mark all of my prayers "slightly imperfect" too. This side of heaven, our prayers together will always fall woefully short of the humility, agreement, and faith that God commends. And yet God who is rich in grace accepts and blesses them because of Christ. Brothers and sisters, "we always find a better welcome with him than we can expect."[15]

Our promise-keeping God assures us that in response to his people's united prayers, he is pleased to heal the sick, save the lost, open prison gates, revive his people, and lovingly grant all kinds of requests. What better incentive do we need?

PART 2

THE FRUITS OF
PRAYING TOGETHER

4

Love

I was nineteen when I attended my first prayer meeting at the small, rural, Pennsylvania church near my college. Five hundred miles from home and remembering the praying fellowship of my childhood, I descended to the church basement one Wednesday night and sat by myself waiting for the meeting to begin. At a long table, two farmers and their wives debated superior tomato varieties. Next to them, an elderly couple smiled cheerfully in their matching square-dance outfits. A man arrived by himself, explaining that his wife's mental illness was preventing her from getting out of bed. A pair of frazzled moms preceded the middle-aged Welsh pastor, and he shut the door.

I almost didn't go back. Every person in that room was at least fifteen years older than me, and some were closer to fifty. They were married, they had kids, they even had grandkids. While I was parsing lines of Chaucer and Spenser, they were plowing rows of soil. While I was thinking about Difficult Questions, their difficulties had moved in and unpacked. While I was planning The Future, they were planning dinner. What could we possibly have in common?

But, by God's grace, I did go back. And Wednesday after

Wednesday, we prayed together. In humble dependence on our common Lord, united in the common work of prayer, and burdened by our common concerns, those saints and I were drawn close. After a few weeks, we were friends; after a few months, family. Though I long ago graduated and moved, I still pray for them today.

In this middle section of the book, we will consider three fruits of praying together: love, discipleship, and revival. In this chapter, our focus will be on how praying together stirs up our love for other Christians. We'll see how corporate prayer paves the way for mutual love by both humbling us and affording us equal usefulness. Then we'll examine the common cause which unites us in prayer. Finally, we'll see how love flourishes when we come together to carry one another's burdens to the Lord. In the words of one nineteenth-century prayer-meeting manual: "We should become better and better acquainted with the household of faith, and discover, perhaps to our astonishment, with what very amiable people our lot has been cast."[1]

On Our Knees

My parents' church has kneelers under its pews, and the congregation uses them during prayer.[2] When we worshiped there recently, I noticed that kneeling is a great equalizer. My husband stands 6'4" tall, but on his knees he seemed about the same as everyone else. Next to him, my kids got a boost from the padded surface and appeared taller than usual. Looking around the room, I watched petite grandmas straighten up and lanky athletes bend down. On our knees, we were leveled.

Whether or not we physically kneel, praying together makes way for mutual love by bringing us all into the same position. "So," writes Paul, "if there is any encouragement in Christ, any comfort from love, any participation in the Spirit, any affection and sympathy, complete my joy by being of the same mind, having the same love, being in full accord and of one mind. Do nothing from selfish ambition or conceit, but in humility count others more significant than yourselves" (Phil. 2:1–3). Pride is the enemy of love. Humility is its best friend.

When we pray together, we pray in the humility of faith. We each come to prayer precisely because we are weak, needy, and sinful. We possess only what Thomas Manton called "the empty hand of the soul . . . [which] looketh for all from God."[3] A company of praying people is a company of people equally dependent on God. But we also come to prayer with equally good help. The most eloquent spiritual giant and the most timid new believer can pray boldly together because Jesus prays for them both.

Not only does praying together remind us that we are equally needy and equally welcome before the throne; it also assures us that we can be equally useful. Sadly, contemporary Christianity is plagued by unbiblical elitism. We esteem Christians who *do* stuff. An academic who formulates Big Ideas impacts the world more than a child with Down syndrome. A thirty-year-old who moves to Asia and rescues sex-trafficking victims is doing more for Christ than an elderly widow in a suburban nursing home. We value specialized skill sets and human strength and visible results.

But as it so often does, the Bible challenges our priorities. Listen to Paul's report to the Colossian church:

Epaphras, who is one of you, a servant of Christ Jesus, greets you, always struggling on your behalf in his prayers, that you may stand mature and fully assured in all the will of God. For I bear him witness that he has worked hard for you and for those in Laodicea and in Hierapolis. (Col. 4:12–13)

Epaphras was doing extremely valuable work for the Lord. It was a constant struggle. It required a sacrifice of time and energy. It encouraged the saints and helped three different churches. It was really, really hard. He was praying in a prayer meeting.

Scripture commends Epaphras as a laborer in corporate prayer. Though praying together might not look like much to our results-driven culture, the Bible assures us that work is getting done. When we pray, we call upon the God who convicts, converts, sanctifies, emboldens, empowers, and protects. When we pray, important things are happening.

And all of God's people can participate. As John Owen wrote, "The prayers of the meanest saints may be useful to the greatest apostle."[4] We are healthy. We are sick. We are male. We are female. We are young. We are elderly. We are rich and poor and solidly middle-income. We are all valuable laborers. In 1859 in Scotland, the Lord graciously sent revival. And in one community, it began through the work of a woman with disabilities:

> In Burghead, one of the fishing villages of the North . . . at a prayer-meeting, held in the house of a Christian woman, laid for the last thirty years on a bed of affliction, the burden of prayers, at her request, was for the outpouring of the Spirit, for the quickening of God's people and the conversion of sinners. Ere long the careless fishing people were awakened, and many of them converted to the Lord; while the entire community, with few exceptions, was moved, and not a few, formerly without the pale of the church, came forward to confess the faith.[5]

Because a woman who had not left her house for decades asked her friends to come over and pray, the Lord moved the course of an entire town.

We should also remember that it's not just the one who prays aloud who does the work. While one person speaks, we all labor together with them in prayer, adding our "Amen" to their words. Perhaps one of the most loving things we can do is to pray together with saints who cannot pray aloud themselves. In my own life, I have done real kingdom work with those whose minds have been crippled by illness and with those for whom words of prayer are physically impossible. I have wrapped my arms around a woman in a mental-health facility, praying aloud while she simply nodded.

I have prayed alongside elderly Alzheimer's patients and people dying of cancer—those for whom spoken prayer will not happen again until they bless Jesus to his face. I have prayed, too, in the company of unborn children with the sincere hope that they might, like John the Baptist, leap in praise though they cannot speak. When we pray out loud alongside those who cannot, we pray *for* them—sharing our words when they have none of their own—and we pray *with* them—valuing their silent spiritual work as certainly as Christ values it, too. On our knees together, we are leveled.

Band of Brothers

Not only our common position of humility, but also our goal in prayer—the common cause of Christ and his kingdom—unites us in mutual affection. In William Shakespeare's *Henry V* the English soldiers assemble on St. Crispin's Day, outnumbered five to one before the Battle of Agincourt. They are bedraggled but loyal, and Henry stirs them to battle by reminding them that they are united in a common cause against a common enemy and promising them each an equal share in the glory. Henry describes for his men the king and the peasant fighting side by side, and his triumphant words—"We few, we happy few, we band of brothers"[6]—draw the soldiers together. So, too, when we engage in spiritual battle in prayer, we are a band of brothers. Not only are we all useful in the work; we are all working for the same thing.

In prayer together, we are all loyal subjects of the same king. When we walk into a prayer meeting and hear others praying words of deep affection for our God, we are instantly among friends. Our unity with and love for other Christians is so rooted in Christ's love for us and our love for him (Eph. 3:14–19) that any friend of Jesus is a friend of ours.

One of our first priorities in corporate prayer ought to be praying for the local church as a whole: for her holiness, unity, boldness, protection, and growth. If we forgo this, our times of prayer together can become simply a list of individual concerns. To be clear: praying together for individual needs is both loving and necessary, and we will consider it later in this chapter. But in our enthusiasm for particular situations, we must never neglect to pray for the cause of the whole church. This is the pattern of the prayer our Lord taught us to pray: "Your kingdom come, your will be done" (Matt. 6:10). Praying together for the entire body helps us to avoid partiality, keeping us from praying only for individuals whom we know well or only individuals whose needs are outward and obvious to us.[7] When believers unite in prayer for Christ's bride, no one is preferred and no one is forgotten.

After Peter and John were imprisoned and then released, the early church met together for prayer. A specific instance of persecution against specific members of the church led the believers to pray for the whole church, "Grant to your servants to continue to speak your word with all boldness" (Acts 4:29). And the Lord's answer to them transformed the whole church: "They were all filled with the Holy Spirit and continued to speak the word of God with boldness" (v. 31). Bold members grew bolder, timid members found new courage, and everyone was remembered before the Lord. When we pray for the whole church, we lovingly unite in a common cause for the common good.

Out of our love for one another then, we overflow in love toward others outside our praying group. First, we turn our mutual love in prayer toward the church in other places—and in the process we grow in love for her.[8] "Help us by prayer," writes Paul to a distant congregation (2 Cor. 1:11). Praying together for the saints in other places reminds us that God is not working only in our community or in our church. God is working everywhere his people meet. This truth is both humbling and encouraging. Is God evident in our midst? He is also working elsewhere at the same time. We have no monopoly on the power of the gospel. Does God seem distant from our local body? But he is even now advancing the cause of his name in other places—among other people who are joined to us through Christ.

One of my sons, when he was about five years old, went through a period of praying nightly in family worship for "the Christians in Bosnia and Herzegovina." I don't know why that country occurred to him—I suspect it was the tongue-twisting possibilities of its name—but night by night he faithfully remembered those Christians before God's throne, and we found our hearts increasingly drawn to them. Today, I can't look at a map or hear a news story from that region without offering a prayer on behalf of the church there. In heaven, I want to be present when my son meets the Bosnian and Herzegovinian saints and hears them tell what his prayers accomplished. We share in God's work throughout the world when we obey his command to pray together for all saints everywhere (Eph. 6:18; 1 Tim. 2:1).

Second, our mutual love turns outward even to our enemies. Satan and his demons are our spiritual enemies, of course, but we also have flesh-and-blood enemies in this world. Christians don't go looking for enemies; as far as it depends on us, we seek to live at peace with all men (Rom. 12:18). Our enemies are therefore not personal nemeses. Our enemies are those who "set themselves . . . against the LORD and against his Anointed" (Ps. 2:2). Our enemies are those who ridicule, attack, hurt, or kill God's people because of Christ. And the one who sets himself against our Lord sets himself against all of us.

This formula—people joining together against a corporate enemy—may seem familiar. In our day, in the name of Allah and Islam, religious people frequently unite against their perceived enemies. In the name of solidarity, they do violence. But Christ prescribes for his followers something much more radical: "Love your enemies and pray for those who persecute you" (Matt. 5:44). We love other Christians in prayer, and our love extends even to our enemies. Why? Because we know from personal experience that God delights to make his enemies his friends. We ourselves were once his enemies, and now we are his beloved. So we gather in united prayer for our enemies—for those who would shame the name of Christ and all who belong to him—not primarily that they might be shamed, but that they would be reconciled to our God. This is made explicit in 1 Timothy 2:1–4 when God commands prayer "for all people," even the notoriously antagonistic "kings and all who are in high positions," because he "desires all people to be saved" (vv. 1, 2, 4).[9] We pray that our enemies would share in our love.

During a season of revival in Germany in 1860, the Lord poured out his Spirit at the Elberfeld Orphan Asylum. A group of seven boys began to pray together every night in the orphanage kitchen. Some of their housemates joined them, but others actively persecuted the group. One fourteen-year-old bully, in particular, loudly declared his contempt—"If they are all converted, I will not be"—and went to bed early, telling his fellow scoffers, "While the others are making such a noise with their prayers, we will take a quiet nap!" But in the Lord's kindness, the bully couldn't sleep. He got out of bed and went to the kitchen. Standing at the door, he overheard the other boys praying tenderly for his salvation. That night, the Lord used the loving, united prayer of young boys to make a scoffer God's friend. The next night, the children saw their former enemy join the prayer meeting and lead the group in prayer.[10]

We are a band of brothers. United in love for our common Savior, joined in his common cause of prayer for both friends and enemies, we find our affections kindled and our hearts warmed toward one another.

Face-to-Face

In his book *Spiritual Disciplines within the Church*, Donald Whitney highlights a common contradiction in some Christians' lives: "There are many who are quick to *ask* for prayer from people in the church and who will even pray for others in return, but who will not commit themselves to pray *with* these same brothers and sisters."[11] Whitney wrote those words ten years ago, and I think they are even more perceptive today. Text messaging and social-media platforms make it increasingly easy to ask people to pray *for us* while conveniently distancing us from any obligation to pray *with them*.

Praying together requires selflessness. In corporate prayer we surrender our personal priorities—holding our own checklist of prayer requests loosely while committing ourselves to pray for the needs of other individuals and of the group as a whole. Also, we surrender our own comfort—showing up to a certain place at a particular time among real people.

But this is the way of love. Families, friends, and lovers naturally want to do things together, to see each other's faces and to respond to each other's emotions in real time. As one older writer memorably put it: "The fingers in a mitten warm each other; in a glove they are chilled by separation."[12] Consider David's sadness compounded by distance: "My friends and companions stand aloof from my plague, and my nearest kin stand far off" (Ps. 38:11). Then contrast these "friends" to the apostle Paul. At least seven times in his various epistles,[13] he expresses his longing to be face-to-face with faraway saints, and, with great poignancy, he repeatedly commands those who are privileged to be together to actually *be* together: get nose to nose, match smile for smile, greet one another with a holy kiss.[14] No matter how often Paul prayed *for* them, he also wanted to be *with* them.

Togetherness is so important that when we pray with others, Jesus himself promises to be in our midst, praying alongside us (Matt. 18:20). When we are together we can see the joys and sorrows and needs of our brothers and sisters written on their faces and in the set of their shoulders. We can hear it in their voices and feel it in the pressure of their handshakes. When we are together, they can notice these things in us too. Prayer may be an invisible force in the heavenly places, but praying together has a tangible dimension, and there love flourishes.

Bearing Our Burdens

United in this work, shoulder-to-shoulder before the throne of grace, we then fulfill the Lord's commands to share the concerns of our brothers and sisters: "Rejoice with those who rejoice, weep with those who weep" (Rom. 12:15) and "Bear one another's burdens" (Gal. 6:2). Look around you, the Lord says. Is your brother joyful? You should give thanks alongside him. Is your sister grieving? Lament with her. Does someone have a need? It should become your burden too. This is so much more than a token sympathy card or a celebratory bunch of balloons. In prayer together, we join in the praises and laments and supplications of our neighbor, bearing his burdens to the throne, lending him a hand to cast them on the Lord.

Brothers and sisters, in prayer together we love one another.

In the first place, our common experiences are an opportunity for mutual love, and hearing the prayers of sympathetic friends gives us comfort. We take this same comfort from Christ as he prays for us. The one who makes intercession can sympathize with us because he also was tempted, betrayed, hungry, tired, misunderstood, and falsely accused (see Heb. 4:15). Our Jesus was once equally frail, bound by space and time, required to pay taxes, and subject to death. He can also rejoice with us because he, too, has the breath of life, the love of friends, and the help of the Spirit. He has a bride and children and a home. The prayers Jesus is praying for us and alongside us are infinitely loving because he understands.

My husband and I lost our first child through miscarriage on a Wednesday afternoon. That night, we felt the love of Christ in the church prayer meeting. One by one, the saints tenderly carried us to the throne, saints who had themselves experienced miscarriage, infertility, or the death of a child. They lamented and pleaded with the Lord as fellow sufferers, friends who knew our sorrows intimately and whose prayers testified to their own experience of God's certain grace. When, a year later, the Lord gave us a son, the saints prayed again, this time in shared celebration—every one of them who had a son or a nephew, everyone who taught school or volunteered in the nursery, everyone who had ever tickled a baby's tiny toes, understood our joy and participated in it by prayer.

But perhaps even more, Christians feel the love of Christ in the body when we hear other saints praying fervently for things they have *not* experienced. We who are sitting on comfortable couches around a warm fire "remember those who are in prison, as though in prison with them, and those who are mistreated, since you also are in the body" (Heb. 13:3). When our brothers and sisters are imprisoned by persecution and also by sorrow, sin, illness, material need, and hope deferred, we pray as if chained with them. Healthy members pray for the sick, wealthy members pray for the needy, and mature members pray for the immature "since you also are in the body."

We share, too, in others' blessings. We rejoice together in prayer and defeat covetousness by having "such a charitable frame of the whole soul toward our neighbor, as that all our inward motions and affections touching him, tend unto, and further all that good which is his."[15] Is our brother rejoicing? Not only do we celebrate with him, but we "further all that good"—asking that he would have even more of a good thing. Sick members pray for the healthy, needy members pray for the wealthy, and immature members pray for the mature "since you also are in the body."

I clearly remember the hot July evening when I sat in a prayer meeting and listened as a divorced, single mom of three brought before the Lord the names of church couples engaged to be married. She laid them tenderly before the Lord, pleading blessings for them that she herself had not received: joy, faithfulness, kindness. She begged God on behalf of these bright, naïve young people, and she asked that their happiness might be multiplied. This is love.

As a pastor's wife, I sometimes hear people lament their experience in the local church: I don't have any friends. I don't think people know me. I don't feel plugged in. I don't feel loved. My suggestion to them is simple. Please come to the church prayer meeting, I tell them. Come and pray on Tuesdays with Carol and me, I say. Come over to our house for dinner and family worship, I say. If you come, you will find work to do and people to love.

Brothers and sisters, we need each other. We need to work together, to know and be known, to love each other by prayer. Please come.

Circle of Love

We have seen that praying together begets love. By humility and hard work, by joining in a common cause, by investing ourselves in the joys and sorrows of others, we grow in love for one another. But we also find in Scripture that love begets praying together. Hear Paul's prayer for the church: "May the God of endurance and encouragement grant you to live in such harmony with one another, in accord with Christ Jesus, that together you may with one voice glorify the God and Father of our Lord Jesus Christ" (Rom. 15:5–6). In a glorious circle, as we love each other we cultivate one harmonious voice—with which we delight to pray together all the more.

5

Discipleship

You probably learned to pray by praying with someone else. Maybe it was a parent whose mealtime and bedtime words of thanks and supplication still shape your prayers to this day. Maybe it was a pastor whose fervent praise from the pulpit first opened your eyes to the priority of delighting in God by prayer. Maybe it was a friend, someone who led you—phrase by phrase—in your first halting prayer of repentance and faith as you began your new life as a Christian. Praying together is a school for prayer.

But whether you realized it or not, those praying saints taught you more than just a method for prayer. By praying with you, they modeled for you what faith looks like, and they stirred you to greater faith. In even the briefest moments of calling on the name of the Lord, they reminded you of who God is and who you are before him. And by prompting you to pray, they helped you to overcome doubt, to withstand temptation, and to reject apostasy. With all heads bowed and all eyes closed, they showed you what it means to be a Christian.

In the last chapter, we saw how we grow in love toward others as we pray with them. In this chapter, we will see how praying together is a loving act of Christian discipleship. The Bible—God's inspired, inerrant, infallible, and authoritative Word—is our only rule for a life of godliness. Discipleship never happens apart from the Scriptures, but it is an invaluable application of them. While we watch and learn, our Christian brothers and sisters take up the materials and the instructions of God's Word and put them to use in the specific, real-time scenarios of life. In the words of one nineteenth-century author: "There cannot be a more brotherly office than to help one another in our prayers, and to excite our mutual devotion."[1]

Throughout my childhood, my father prayed every morning in the living room. If my brother and I got up very early and tip-toed downstairs, we could see him: glasses laid aside, shoulders hunched, head bowed, on his knees beside the couch. It was an awe-inspiring sight. In the quiet, solitary hours before anyone else in the world was awake, our dad was doing something holy.

We learned a valuable lesson from those occasional predawn glimpses of a godly man in private, daily prayer—prayer is important. But it was when our dad prayed *with* us—at bedtimes and mealtimes, in family worship and in church—that we learned the most. There, his prayers were no silent, seemingly mysterious ritual; they were real communication within a real relationship. When we all prayed together, we could hear the evidence for ourselves: our dad actually knew God.

As David Clarkson wrote: "In private [worship] you provide for your own good, but in public you do good both to yourselves and others."[2] In praying together we disciple one another: we strengthen one another's faith, testify to our experiences of God, shape one another's repentance and desires, stir one another to thanksgiving, and encourage one another in godly habits. In these things, too, we also help one another to resist various temptations to sin.

Brothers and sisters, praying together is a school for the whole Christian life.

Training in Faith

The first lesson we learn when we pray with others is not about ourselves, or about our prayers, but about our God. And the most basic element of this lesson is faith—faith that the triune God is a God who loves to hear the prayers and praises of his people. This is the crux of true prayer, according to the writer to the Hebrews: "Without faith it is impossible to please him, for whoever would draw near to God must believe that he exists and that he rewards those who seek him" (Heb. 11:6). At its heart, prayer is an invisible act of faith in an unseen God, and praying with others strengthens our own faith and silences our nagging doubts.

At the tomb of Lazarus, Jesus himself prayed with confidence in the listening Father: "Jesus lifted up his eyes and said, 'Father, I thank you that you have heard me'" (John 11:41). Why did he pray that way? Partly, it was to do good to others by strengthening their faith. He continues, "I knew that you always hear me, but I said this on account of the people standing around, that they may believe that you sent me" (v. 42). Jesus wanted his prayer to be an instrument of discipleship in the lives of others. He wanted to increase their faith.

We certainly learn this lesson in faith by praying with more mature believers, but even the first ragged cry of a newborn Christian trains our hearts to trust God more. If someone has true faith, no matter his abilities, he can be useful in public prayer, because the very act of prayer proclaims the importance of faith. As Isaac Watts wrote, "By expressing the joys of our faith to God, we may often be made a means, through the power of the Holy Spirit, to raise the faith and joy of others."[3] For all of us, hearing the prayers of others is an opportunity for our discipleship.

One Scottish pastor in the 1740s gave this report on the children in his community:

There is also a meeting of themselves [children] in the school-house after the evening exercises, where some hours are spent in prayer to their own edification, and, in some cases, to the conviction of persons standing and listening at the doors and windows. . . . O, how pleasant it is to have the poor young lambs addressing themselves to God in prayer! Sometimes standing outside the room, listening, I am myself often melted into tears.[4]

Can you see it? The schoolkids praying, their parents and teachers pressing ears to the door, wiping tears from their eyes. These children are unlikely to have been excellent pray-ers in the sense of being particularly eloquent or especially knowledgeable in doctrine. But their words of faith in an unseen God and their confidence in his relational inclination to hear them, moved even adults to conviction of sin and to greater faith of their own.

By praying together, we form a cloud of witnesses, engaged together in real communication to our God and testifying to the truth of what we believe. This guards us against the danger of doubt. Calling together on "our Father in heaven" (Matt. 6:9) we proclaim our certainty of his existence and his promise to hear us. In a world that scoffs at the notion of God, or reduces him to something less than he is, we desperately need the prayerful public faith of our Christian brothers and sisters. And should we be tempted to forsake Christ altogether, the cloud of witnesses will remind us of the faith we professed in prayer.

On my own, I can be tempted to think that my prayers rise no higher than the ceiling. But among the gathered saints, among those whose genuine faith is breathed out in their prayers, my own faith is strengthened. My eyes are taken off myself, turned toward my gracious God, and, in the precious words of the Heidelberg Catechism, I am reminded: "It is even more sure that God listens to my prayers than that I really desire what I pray for."[5]

Training in Theology (God-Knowing)
Prayer, as we saw in chapter 1, is an activity based on a relationship. As Christians, our theology (knowledge of God) is no mere

brainteaser. The Puritans frequently talked about "experimental religion," meaning that each believer experiences real communion with God in his own soul. Christianity is rich in doctrine, and that doctrine expresses itself in relationship. When we pray with others then, we glimpse real and ongoing relationships to God. "Come and hear, all you who fear God," writes David in Psalm 66, "and I will tell what he has done for my soul" (v. 16).

In praying with others, we are discipled in the gospel. During my childhood (and to this day) when my dad prayed with me, he prayed to the listening Father, in the name of the Son, by the help of the indwelling Spirit. He prayed as a sinner who had been saved by grace through faith. He prayed as someone who was once willfully ignorant of God but who now knew and loved him as Creator, Redeemer, and Lord. In my dad's prayers, God's gracious character was revealed to me.

When Mary received the blessing of becoming the mother of Jesus, she responded in praise (Luke 1:46–55). She magnified God (v. 46) and rejoiced in his kindness (v. 47), she delighted in the God who blessed her (vv. 48–49), and she praised him as the one who exalts the lowly and humbles the proud (vv. 51–53). Her knowledge of God was intimate and personal, while at the same time being doctrinally rich. How did Mary know what God was like? She learned it, at least in part, from hearing someone else pray. Hundreds of years before Mary conceived the Son of God, the Lord opened the womb of another godly woman—Hannah—and she too responded to God's blessing with public prayer (1 Sam. 2:1–10). Hannah's prayer—delighting in God's blessing (v. 1) and savoring his merciful and gracious kindness toward the lowly (vv. 4–8)—was undoubtedly Mary's school of theology. Because of the prayer of Hannah, when Mary was similarly blessed, she knew exactly what kind of God had blessed her.

Praying together teaches us to know our God. And the personal, experiential nature of those prayers keeps us from spiritual coldness. Hearing the prayers of Hannah and Mary and our parents and the man and the woman in the next pew shows us that our God is intimately at work in the lives of his saints, every day revealing his grace in our salvation, every day condescending to relationship with the lowly and humble. In the company of God's gathered people at prayer, each one rejoicing in God her Savior, our hearts are stirred to love him more.

Samuel Miller gives an account of a minister who prayed during a service with "importunate, touching devotion." Afterward a woman stopped on her way out the door to remark, "That man prays as if he lived at the Throne of grace."[6] I suspect that many of us do not know it is possible to live at the throne of grace until we pray with someone who does. Then we discover that we want to move there too.

Training in Repentance

In the opening of his *Institutes*, John Calvin wrote, "Nearly all the wisdom we possess, that is to say, true and sound wisdom, consists of two parts: the knowledge of God and of ourselves."[7] God-knowing and self-knowing are inseparably linked. Meditating on God's holiness reveals the depths of our sin; viewing our sin exposes our need for the Savior. Knowing God teaches us, like Isaiah, that we need a cleansing coal from the altar (Isa. 6:5). In this way, we move in prayer from knowing God to repenting of sin, and in our repentance, too, we disciple one another.

When we pray together, we practice three types of confession and repentance. First, we confess corporate sins corporately. That is, gathered together, we confess the corporate sins of our local body of believers and of the wider church. We find an example of this in Ezra 9–10: "All who trembled at the words of the God of Israel" (9:4) gathered to confess the sin of the covenant people who had intermarried with pagans. Not every individual Israelite was guilty of this sin, but the godly admitted their connection to those who were and confessed this sin because they were part of the same covenant community. In our day, we might together confess the disunity in our local church, the neglect of gospel proclamation in many corners of our nation's churches, or the pervasive sins of pride, racism, and spiritual apathy in the church worldwide.

Second, we confess individual sins corporately. That is, gathered together, we confess categories of sins that each of us has committed in some way. This is what the Israelites did in the days of Josiah (2 Chron. 34:8–33): the law was read out, all the people humbled themselves, and each one covenanted to follow the Lord "with all his heart and all his soul" (v. 31). In our churches, we might read through the Ten Commandments (Ex. 20:1–17) and together confess that we have broken the law in our own lives.

Finally, we confess individual sins individually. That is, a single individual confesses in the hearing of the group a specific way he has broken God's law. We find this in the book of James: "Therefore, confess your sins to one another and pray for one another, that you may be healed" (James 5:16). Though this command might bring to mind a group-therapy session—with each member disclosing his private struggles—that is not likely to be what James had in mind. Instead, this verse requires us to confess *to* one another the sins we have committed *against* one another, and to pray together for forgiveness and reconciliation.[8] Like Zacchaeus repenting of his fraud and pledging to return the spoils of his sin to its rightful owners (Luke 19:8), we publicly confess the ways we have cheated and wronged those with whom we pray.

In January 1907, in what is now North Korea, a group of 1,500 Christians met for preaching and prayer. As they prayed together, the Spirit convicted them of sins they had committed against one other and moved them to confession. Previously estranged Christians fell side by side on their knees, reconciled in prayer together. Afterward, when returning to their homes in Pyongyang, they took repentance with them: "All through the city men were going from house to house, confessing to individuals they had injured, returning stolen property and money, not only to Christian but to heathen as well, till the whole city was stirred."[9]

In our prayer together we can foster repentance. During family prayer, a father might confess his harshness toward his children (Eph. 6:4). During a church prayer meeting, a member might confess her neglect of worship, which deprived the local body of her vital encouragement (Heb. 10:25). Spouses confess unkind words, coworkers confess unethical practices, and church elders confess failure to submit to one another. Having heard the prayerful confessions of others, we then join together to pray for them—and for ourselves—that we might be restored to communion with a holy God and with one another.

In confession together, we disciple one another by exposing sins that we each ought to confess, by modeling godly repentance and by pointing one another to Christ, the only hope for sinners. Moreover, confessing together is an antidote to pride. Perhaps the chief danger in praying together is that of pride—in our own supposed righteousness (Luke 18:9), in our pretty language (Matt. 6:7), and in our display of piety (Matt. 6:5)—and acknowledging our sin is one God-given cure. There is no room for boasting when we each echo the tax collector's prayer, "God, be merciful to me, a sinner!" (Luke 18:13).

Training in Desire

The first time Carol asked me to come over to pray, I had no idea how it would change me. They say the best way to learn a foreign language is by immersion—move somewhere and listen as the people speak their language in all the ordinary situations of life. From that first Tuesday morning, the years of praying with Carol became a kind of immersion for me, not just in the language of the soul but in the very life of the soul. Never once did Carol directly instruct me: Desire this. Ask for this. Expect this. Instead, she prayed God-centered, Scripture-rich prayers that petitioned God for the things he had promised. And immersed in prayer with her, the things she wanted naturally shaped my own desires too.

Contemporary culture recoils against the idea that our desires can be trained. In the modern world, a person's sexual, financial, relational, and professional aspirations and desires are sacrosanct. Nobody can tell me what I should want. Our desires are seen as highly personal. What's desirable to me is not necessarily desirable to someone else. But the Bible gives us an entirely different picture: God tells us what to want, he bids us to ask him for it, and he promises to answer.

If prayer is "an offering up of our desires unto God, for things agreeable to his will,"[10] then there is a necessary correlation between what God wants, what we want, and what we ask for. Our desires can be—must be!—trained by God's desires. Jonathan Edwards famously said, "Undoubtedly that which God does abundantly make the subject of his promises, God's people should abundantly make the subject of their prayers."[11] What God has promised to do, we should together ask him to do.

We have a beautiful example of this in the book of Acts. At his ascension into heaven, Jesus promised his disciples, "You will receive power when the Holy Spirit has come upon you, and you will be my witnesses in Jerusalem and in all Judea and Samaria, and to the end of the earth" (Acts 1:8). This is God's will: to send the Holy Spirit and to make the church his witness in the world. And so the disciples made it their desire as well, encouraging one another in the same petitions. We find them "with one accord . . . devoting themselves to prayer" for the coming Holy Spirit (v. 14). Later, they "lifted their voices together to God" (4:24), requesting boldness in gospel proclamation. What God had promised, they desired.

In this way, praying with others shapes our desires. On my own, I might be inclined to ask for my own desire: a new house, a comfortable life, a sunny day. In the company of God's people, all crying out with one accord for the things God has promised, I am trained by God's desire. This, then, guards us against sin. "Each person is tempted," says James, "when he is lured and enticed by his own desire" (James 1:14). On its own, the warped desires of a sinner lead inevitably to sin, but desires shaped by the will of God, and encouraged by the right desires of others, lead to righteousness.

Training in Thankfulness

When I was growing up, it was my church's practice to hold an annual thanksgiving service. We pulled those avocado-green vinyl chairs into a semicircle around the piano. We sang a hymn or two. We prayed. And then everyone was given an opportunity to stand up and give thanks to God for specific instances of his kindness over the past year. I remember people's thanks for new babies, new jobs, and new houses. I remember gratitude for physical and spiritual health. I remember tears of joy over sinners who repented and covenant children who made profession of faith. The Lord had done great things for us, and we were glad.

Remembering together who God is and what he has done trains our hearts in thankfulness. This has always been the practice of God's covenant people. In Deuteronomy 29, for example, Moses leads the Israelites to remember God's deliverance from Egypt and his faithfulness in the wilderness where "your clothes have not worn out on you, and your sandals have not worn off your feet" (v. 5). And throughout the psalms, the psalmists call the people to remember aloud God's kind dealings with them in the past:

> Give thanks to the Lord of lords,
>   for his steadfast love endures forever . . .
> to him who struck down the firstborn of Egypt,
>   for his steadfast love endures forever;
> and brought Israel out from among them,
>   for his steadfast love endures forever. (Ps. 136:3, 10–11)

While private moments of gratitude to God are certainly appropriate, thanksgiving is most properly a public event. "To thank God," writes David W. Pao, "is to remember and recount his mighty deeds. Thanksgiving therefore moves beyond the sphere of private sentiments to the public acknowledgement of the mighty and faithful God."[12] In prayer together, we remember what we might otherwise have forgotten, we delight in God's mighty acts toward his covenant people, and we loudly proclaim our thanks.

Thanking God together is an effective guard against ingratitude. On our own, we may be tempted to forget, to take for granted, and to ignore the God from whom every good and perfect gift comes (James 1:17). On our own, we may fall into the ways of the ungodly, who do not "honor him as God or give thanks to him" (Rom. 1:21). Together, though, surrounded by the thanks of others, we join in and are thankful.

Training in Prayer

At the beginning of this chapter, I made the statement that praying together is more than just a school for prayer. As we have seen, praying together trains our hearts in faith, in Christian experience, and in repentance, desire, and thanksgiving. It is not merely a school for prayer, but it certainly *is* a school for prayer.

The habit of praying reverently, clearly, and biblically is often learned in the hearing of others. First, we are compelled to pray with reverence. Praying is a serious task—we approach the Most High God, who promises to use our prayers to accomplish great things. Praying together is an even greater incentive to reverence, because we take others by the hand and bring them to the throne with us. Second, if we expect others to enter into our prayers and say "Amen"—and we do! (1 Cor. 14:16)—we have a responsibility to pray carefully. For everyone's sake, we must pray clearly, knowing what we are asking and from whom we ask it. And we must pray biblically, evaluating our public prayers against the measure of God's Word.

Praying together also fosters a habit of praying regularly, guarding us against the sin of prayerlessness. I am most inclined to pray privately either when I feel close to the Lord or when I encounter some urgent need. I am fervent in prayer when a crisis or a decision or an illness looms large, fervent in prayer when my Bible reading is especially precious, fervent in prayer when my heart is warmed and my (perceived) needs are great. However, on an ordinary Tuesday morning I may not be all that inclined to prayer, so my habit of praying with others guarantees that I still pray regularly. On Sundays I pray multiple times with the gathered church, on Tuesdays I pray with a group of women and also with my husband, on Wednesdays I pray with the church again, and every morning and every evening I pray with my family. Whether I feel like it or not, I pray.

Are You Ready?

Earlier this week I met to pray with two older women in my church. We discussed a few matters for prayer—a new gospel podcast for Arabic-speaking millennials, a paralyzed Christian sister, the labors of our pastor—and then we sat quietly. After a moment one of the women said, with a sparkle in her eyes, "Sisters, are you ready?" Her enthusiasm stirred my heart. And, as if embarking on an epic adventure, we all smiled, straightened our shoulders, and began to pray together.

I can think of no better—or simpler—discipleship program than for more mature and less mature believers to sit diligently under the preaching of the Word and then to pray together. I can also think of nothing more exciting. This was how you first learned the faith, this was how the members of the early church grew (Acts 2:42), this is how Christ is even now conforming to himself the saints in Korea and the saints in my own church, and it is how those around you will come to maturity too.

Brothers and sisters, are you ready?

6

Revival

In 1858 God poured out his Spirit in an extraordinary measure, first in New York, then throughout the United States. This revival was the occasion of the strengthening of churches and the conversion of many thousands of souls. It affected people of all ages, races, socioeconomic conditions, and church denominations. It was so widely felt that even the secular newspapers of the time published regular reports of it. And it began at a prayer meeting attended by seven people. In his firsthand account of the spiritual events of that year, the minister Samuel Prime wrote: "This revival is to be remembered through all coming ages as simply an answer to prayer."[1]

So far in this book, we have focused almost entirely on prayer itself. We have considered the biblical foundations of praying together: divine and human relationship, our duty, and God's promises. We have also savored the fruits of mutual love and discipleship that grow as we pray together. But now, and before moving on to engage the practical details of praying together, we will turn our attention to a slightly different kind of fruit—namely, God's answer to our prayer.

The answers to our prayers are as varied as the prayers themselves. In the book of James alone, we learn that God answers prayer by healing sick saints (5:14–16), by withholding and sending rain (5:17–18), by giving wisdom (1:5), and by granting all kinds of good requests that come from a pure heart (1:17; 4:2–3). Only eternity will fully reveal the myriad of loving answers, both large and small, that God gave in response to his people's supplications.

In a book about praying together, it is appropriate for us to particularly consider one of the greatest of all God's answers, that most glorious corporate blessing he has often been pleased to give his gathered people as they pray: revival.

Stacks of books have been written on revival: its theological foundations, its historic occurrences, and its implications for Christians today.[2] In the brief space of this chapter, we will not attempt an exhaustive study but rather focus on revival as a fruit of praying together. We will consider first what revival is, then two biblical incentives to pray together for it, and finally how corporate prayer and revival intertwine—each flowing from and leading to the other.

What Is Revival?

I suspect we have all participated in a prayer meeting in which it was not quite clear what, exactly, we were asking God to do. Perhaps we were praying for "traveling mercies," or "blessing on this situation," or for God to "be with" so-and-so. Those things sound good. But what are we really asking, why do we think God wants us to ask for that, and would we even recognize the answer if God said yes? For many of us, I think revival is another one of those fuzzy-around-the-edges blessings that we are quick to pray for and slow to understand. Sure, we pray for revival. Revival sounds great. But what exactly is it?

J. I. Packer provides a helpful definition. Summarizing Jonathan Edwards's significant work on the subject, Packer writes: "Revival is an extraordinary work of God the Holy Ghost reinvigorating and propagating Christian piety in a community."[3] In order to better understand revival—and to ask God for it with greater confidence—we will examine and apply this definition one phrase at a time.

Here, we notice first that revival is the work of the Holy Spirit. The Spirit—given by the Father and the Son—empowers the Word (1 Thess. 1:5), convicts of sin (John 16:8), gives new life (John 3:6), helps us to pray (Rom. 8:26), opens our lips to sing God's praises (Eph. 5:18–19), enables new obedience (Rom. 8:4), and manifests his fruit in our lives (Gal. 5:22–23). Revival is God's work and, therefore, is under God's sovereign power. He brings it when, where, and how he pleases according to the purpose of his will. He does it, as he does everything, for his own glory. And he does it in a manner consistent with his unchanging character. Revival, from beginning to end, is something only God can do.

For this reason, it is especially appropriate that we make revival a subject for prayer. Prayer is an admission of need, asking God to do for us what we cannot do for ourselves, and our most urgent need is for the Holy Spirit.[4] Jesus himself gives us this encouragement: "If you then, who are evil, know how to give good gifts to your children, how much more will the heavenly Father give the Holy Spirit to those who ask him!" (Luke 11:13). And when we pray for the Spirit, we are praying alongside Christ, who asks the Father for the Spirit on our behalf (John 14:16). The Holy Spirit, the divine agent of revival, is a gift that Christ promises to supply when we pray.

Recognizing that revival is the Spirit's sovereign work also keeps us from demanding revival or from thinking that revival hangs on the strength of our prayers. As we noted in chapter 3, Christians can sometimes approach prayer like a math problem, believing that enough people praying with enough boldness will force God to answer in the way we want. Instead, in the words of Ian Murray, "God has chosen to make prayer a *means* of blessing, not so that the fulfilment of his purposes becomes dependent on us, but rather to help us learn *our* absolute dependence upon him."[5] It is essential that we pray together for revival but impossible that we can compel it. We ask humbly, and we await his good answer.

The second thing we notice about revival is that it is an extraordinary work. "Extraordinary" here does not mean new or different, but greater in measure or degree. In the New Testament, the Spirit definitively filled the Christians at Pentecost (Acts 2:4) and then later filled the same Christians again in extra measure (Acts 4:31).[6] When we pray for revival, we are asking the Spirit to do what he usually does ("reinvigorating and propagating Christian piety") and to do more of it. In fact, we might not recognize revival immediately because it looks so much like what the Spirit is already doing. Murray writes, "From Pentecost onward, the work of the Spirit can be viewed in two aspects, the more normal and the extraordinary. These two differ not in essence or kind, but only in degree, so much so that we can never determine with certainty where the normal ends and the extraordinary begins."[7]

In Charles Dickens's classic novel *Oliver Twist*, the title character is sent as a young orphan boy to a workhouse. There he receives a single serving of gruel every night for dinner. After months of the scant ration, Oliver one evening finishes his porridge, gathers his courage, and approaches the workhouse master with his empty bowl and the famous words: "Please sir, I want some more."[8]

We do something similar when we pray for revival. Having experienced the Holy Spirit, having tasted a portion of his presence and his power, we approach the Father with a bold request: Please, sir, may we have some more? But unlike the workhouse master, who met Oliver's request with dramatic incredulity ("'What!' said the master at length in a faint voice"[9]), our gracious God delights to answer our petition with another generous ladling of the Spirit into our churches and our communities.

With this understanding then, we avoid praying for revival as something different, a magic bullet, that bears no resemblance to

God's normal work in our midst. Michael Horton recently critiqued the evangelical desire for revival as a facet of our modern, restless quest for "The Next Big Thing,"[10] and Murray himself points out that "too often in the twentieth century there has been faith in 'revival' where there has been little faith in God himself."[11] But prayer for revival should not be isolated from our prayers for God's glory (Matt. 6:9), for the advancement of Christ's kingdom and obedience to his Word (Matt. 6:10), for the success of gospel preaching (Col. 4:3; 2 Thess. 3:1), for the building up of the church and the tearing down of Satan's dominion (Matt. 16:18), and for sinners' repentance (2 Pet. 3:9). We pray together for revival by praying for God to do his ordinary work—in an extraordinary measure. Brothers and sisters, we ask for more.

Finally, we see that when God answers our prayers for revival, he does it in a community. As Packer explains, revival is a work of the Spirit, it is extraordinary, and it comes to a group of people. This is not to say that God cannot or will not revive individuals; the psalms are full of rich testimony to God's reviving grace in the hearts of particular saints. But just as the Spirit filled the whole church at Pentecost and then added three thousand more to their number (Acts 2:4, 41), revival is most especially God's work on a corporate scale, beginning first in the church and then extending outward to the surrounding community. (We will consider this in greater detail in the next two sections of this chapter.)

And since revival is a corporate blessing, given to the church and to her community, it is especially appropriate that we ask God for it together. This was the pattern of the church in Acts, and it is rightly our pattern, too. As a family, as a student body, as employees, as members of a community, and—especially!—as a church, we gather together to pray for an answer we expect to receive together.

Brothers and sisters, let us pray together in the Spirit for the Spirit,[12] knowing what we are asking and from whom we will receive it.

He Establishes Jerusalem

Having defined revival, we will now consider the two primary characteristics of revival ("reinvigorating" and "propagating" Christian piety) with the specific incentives that the Bible gives us to pray for each of them. In the first place, revival is God reinvigorating his people, the church. The freshly revived church will have right affections—rejecting sin, eagerly attending the preaching of the Word, and being constant in prayer—and she will abound in good works to those in her midst and also outside.[13] This is something God promises to do, and it is something he commands us to pray for:

> On your walls, O Jerusalem,
>   I have set watchmen;
> all the day and all the night
>   they shall never be silent.
> You who put the LORD in remembrance,
>   take no rest,
> and give him no rest
>   until he establishes Jerusalem
>   and makes it a praise in the earth. (Isa. 62:6–7)

In Isaiah 62 God tells us he is going to make his church, here called Jerusalem,[14] righteous (v. 1), beautiful (v. 3), and an object of divine rejoicing (v. 5). She will be nourished without threat from her enemies (vv. 8–9), will be firmly established, and will be "a praise in the earth" (v. 7).

On the strength of his promise, God commands all "who put the LORD in remembrance" (v. 6) to pray for this. Everyone who loves Christ's church must ask him for her establishment.[15] Moreover, we are to pray not just once or twice but without ceasing. We are to take no rest for ourselves. And, in an invitation to divinely sanctioned audacity, God tells us not to give him any rest either. We are to be like the persistent widow who returned again and again with her request (Luke 18:1–8). We are to be like the prophetess

Anna who never left the place of prayer and fasting (Luke 2:37). We are to imitate Paul who prayed for the church at all hours (1 Thess. 3:10). And we are to pray in opposition to the relentless Enemy of the church who accuses her night and day (Rev. 12:10). By divine command, we must pray for the reinvigorating of God's people—morning and evening, today and tomorrow, this year and next year, and in all the years until Christ's return.

One day, when we are beyond time, when Christ returns and we enter into eternity with him, when the new Jerusalem comes down (Rev. 21:2) and is fully and finally established, we will join the cherubim and seraphim and the company of the saints whose praises never cease night and day (Rev. 4:8–11; 7:15). We who gave God no rest on earth, asking for his blessing, will give him no rest in eternity, thanking him for his answer.

Earlier in this chapter, I described the New York revival that started at a prayer meeting begun by a man named Jeremiah Lamphier. Lamphier wrote in his diary: "One day, as I was walking along the streets, the idea was suggested to my mind that an hour of prayer, from twelve to one o'clock would be beneficial to *business men*, who usually in great numbers take that hour for rest and refreshment."[16] That first prayer meeting, held on September 23, 1857, soon expanded to one hundred fifty noon-time meetings throughout the city where, instead of taking a rest, the businessmen of New York gave themselves and their God no rest.[17]

And what an answer they received! Beginning in New York and then throughout the United States, the Lord poured out his Spirit on his people. Samuel Prime reported:

> The changes which came over the church were most welcome. . . . It was a blessed spectacle presented to the world, a church alive, a church active, a church of prayer. It was a sublime spectacle, when this was seen as the moral position, not of one church, but of a majority of churches; not in one place,

but in every place, when all the land seemed to be moved by one common impulse.[18]

Brothers and sisters, let us pray together at all times (Eph. 6:18)—on coffee breaks and lunch breaks, in early mornings and late nights and every snatched moment in between—giving God no rest until he establishes his people.

He Sends Out Laborers

The second characteristic of revival is "propagating Christian piety." In revival, the Spirit's work extends beyond the bounds of the church, regenerating hearts in large numbers. Most of us have never personally witnessed the conversion of masses of people— whether the three thousand on the day of Pentecost (Acts 2:41) or the three hundred thousand during the Great Awakening of 1740–1742 or the fifty thousand every week during the 1858 revival[19]—but we have strong biblical incentive to pray for it. One of our best encouragements comes from Jesus's words to his disciples: "The harvest is plentiful, but the laborers are few. Therefore pray earnestly to the Lord of the harvest to send out laborers into his harvest" (Luke 10:2).

Our prayer for the gospel's success in the hearts of sinners is made urgent by Jesus's use of contrast. On the one hand, we have the promised, glorious, abundant harvest of souls. On the other, we have a meager trickle of laborers heading out to the field. This is not good, says Jesus. I have a vast number, ready to pluck to myself. Don't be satisfied with a single preacher here or there when the world needs a great company. Ask the Father to send more. (It's interesting to note that in this incident Jesus is sending out seventy-two men. By the standards of most of our churches, the commissioning of seventy-two missionaries at one time would be amazing. But Jesus here calls them "few" and says to pray earnestly for more!)

When we pray together for the conversion of many, we pray

alongside Jesus, whom the Father bids, "Ask of me, and I will make the nations your heritage, and the ends of the earth your possession" (Ps. 2:8). We know that the prayers of Christ—and our prayers in harmony with him—will be answered. In heaven we will personally witness the Father's answer in the "great multitude that no one could number, from every nation, from all tribes and peoples and languages, standing before the throne and before the Lamb" (Rev. 7:9). We have every reason to ask God for more—more workers, more redeemed souls in more places, and, ultimately, more glory to the Lamb.

In 1806 a college student named Samuel Mills began to pray for the cause of foreign missions. Up until this time, the missionary organizations that existed in the United States were solely dedicated to domestic missions, both in the Western frontier and among Native American tribes.[20] But at Williams College, Mills prayed that the Lord would raise up and send out men to carry the gospel to other nations. Eventually, he assembled a small group of spiritually minded friends: "He led them out into a meadow, at a distance from the College . . . where by the side of a large stack of hay, he devoted the day to prayer and fasting, and familiar conversation on this new and interesting theme [foreign missions]."[21] Some accounts say there was a sudden thunderstorm as they were praying, which caused the men to take refuge under the haystack.[22] After that day, they continued to gather weekly for what became known as the Haystack Prayer Meeting. In answer to the prayers from among the haystacks, God was pleased to establish the American Board of Commissioners for Foreign Missions, the American Bible Society, and the United Foreign Missionary Society and, through those organizations, to send out many laborers into his ripened harvest field.[23]

Brothers and sisters, let us pray together wherever we can—in back rooms and backyards, in empty classrooms and in deserted stairwells, at picnic tables and pews and subway platforms—asking the Lord to gather a great harvest to himself.

Praying Together and Revival, Revival and Praying Together

As we have seen, revival—the extraordinary Spirit work of reinvigorating and propagating—is often God's answer to his people's united prayer. But praying together does not stop when his gracious answer is received. As we noted in chapter 2, God's people are praying people. God's revived people are even more so—feeling even more deeply the privilege of their relationship to Christ and his church, and taking even more seriously his call to obedience. Praying together may lead to revival. Revival always leads to more praying together.

This glorious circle is evident in the book of Acts. After Jesus's ascension, the believers "with one accord were devoting themselves to prayer" (Acts 1:14). Then the Lord filled them with his Spirit (Acts 2:4) and also regenerated many others (v. 41). Immediately afterward, we find the Christians again devoting themselves to prayer together daily (vv. 42, 46). We then read that "awe came upon every soul" (v. 43), and "the Lord added to their number day by day those who were being saved" (v. 47). This pattern—praying together, the strengthening of the church, the conversion of many, and then praying together again—repeats throughout the history of the church.

During the 1740s, the Spirit brought the Cambuslang Revival in Scotland. The pastor of the church in Cambuslang described how the revival was preceded in February 1742 by the people of his church offering "extraordinary and fervent prayers in large meetings, and particularly in relation to the success of the gospel."[24] Three months later, the newly revived Christians manifested "fervent love to one another; the keeping up of divine worship in families; the setting up of *new meetings for prayer, both of old and young*, partly within the parish, where *twelve such Societies are now begun*, and partly elsewhere, among the awakened."[25] The people prayed together, the Lord revived them and added to their number, and then they prayed together even more.

It is particularly moving to read about the praying children of Cambuslang and its surrounding parishes. The students at one school, some "not more than eight or nine years of age, and others twelve or thirteen,"[26] asked their teacher for permission to hold a prayer meeting at the school. They then prayed together "thrice a day—in the morning, at mid-day, and at night."[27] At another school, "about twenty of them meet twice a week, some of them having a considerable way to travel homeward in the dark."[28] One pastor reported that "about sixteen children in the town were observed to meet together in a barn for prayer."[29] In other towns, "boys were found in the fields engaged in prayer,"[30] and "several girls between ten and fourteen years of age had been observed to meet in an out-house for prayer."[31] In the schoolrooms, barns, fields, and outhouses, the children of Scotland prayed together. Morning, noon, and night they gave the Lord no rest. And with small voices and big prayers, they asked God to give them more. Oh, that today the Lord would pour out his Spirit on the children and the adults in our own communities!

The circle of praying together and revival, revival and praying together, finds its culmination in eternity. Upon Christ's return, the church will be fully and finally established, never to be shaken again. The complete harvest of redeemed souls will be laid with rejoicing in the heavenly barns. And all God's people will be made more alive than they ever were, their bodies and souls permanently glorified. There, that ultimate and unfading revival will give rise to an eternal prayer meeting, and the whole great multitude will praise the Lamb together forever.

PART 3

THE PRACTICE OF PRAYING TOGETHER

7

Praying with the Church

It would not be much of an exaggeration to say that I wrote this entire book just so I could write this chapter. The first two parts of the book, The Foundations of Praying Together and The Fruits of Praying Together, are essential. They are the necessary biblical *why* that constrains our conscience and compels our action. But now, considering the *how*, we approach the particular burden of my heart, the aspect of praying together which has most enriched my own soul and which I believe is most vital—but perhaps most neglected—in the lives of the saints: the local church at prayer.[1]

Here, I will plead for two things: substantial, elder-led prayer in corporate worship and regular, public prayer meetings in church life. In order to facilitate those, I will also address two important, practical issues: first, how to pray while someone else leads and, second, how to lead while others pray.

Brothers and sisters, in the words attributed to Martin Luther, "Let us pray—in the church, with the church, for the church!"[2]

Substantial, Elder-Led Prayer in Corporate Worship

As a teenager I lived for several months in the Scottish Highlands and worshiped with a Free Church of Scotland congregation. I remember my surprise that first Lord's Day when, as the pastor began to pray, the entire church rose to its feet, standing together for the length of the prayer.[3] As I joined them, I was conscious of being part of a group in action. We were not asleep. We were not listening passively to someone else pray. No. We were at worship, at work, and at war. We were the church, and we were praying together.

If we want a local church that prays together (and we do!), we need *substantial, elder-led prayer in corporate worship.* We have already seen in Scripture that praying together is a clear priority of the people of God and that it is specifically and repeatedly given a prominent place in their *corporate worship* (Isa. 56:7; Matt. 21:12–13; 1 Tim. 2:8).[4] In Lord's Day worship, the church is gathered as a visible assembly—the covenant people of God exalting him together for all the world to see. In worship, God speaks to man (through the reading and preaching of Scripture), and man speaks to God (through singing and prayer). We approach the throne not as an assortment of individuals, but as a united people, a single nation, an interconnected and interdependent body. As we pray in corporate worship, we speak to our God with one voice (see Acts 4:24–30).

With this in view, our Lord's Day prayer with the church should have *substantial content.* The pagans might "heap up empty phrases" (Matt. 6:7), but the people of God have weighty matters for prayer. Scripture directs us to pray big prayers together: praise (Ps. 34:3), confession (James 5:16), and thanksgiving (Ps. 100:4), as well as intercession for civil authorities (1 Tim. 2:1–2), for ministry and missions (Matt. 9:37–38), for the salvation of all men (1 Tim. 2:1, 4), for sanctification of God's people (Col. 1:9–12), and for comfort to the afflicted (James 5:13–18).[5] When the church prays, she brings to the throne all the concerns of Christ and his church.

Our prayer with the church should also receive *substantial time.* The full range of our God-directed concerns cannot possibly be prayed in the space of thirty seconds. Also, it requires time for the entire congregation to engage their hearts in prayer. The church is not helped by the prayer leader who blurts out a prayer and then retreats with a fast "Amen," never considering the people in the pews who are still scrambling to find their souls. The Puritans used to say, "Pray until you pray," meaning that prayer is not a quick, mindless ritual to check off the list but a real communication with the living God. So, too, the church must be willing to take the time to pray fully and intentionally. For the sake of God's glory, for the sake of Christ's kingdom, for the sake of the mature believer, the little child, and the curious outsider—pray. Pray until everyone prays. If we truly believe that prayer is the glorious privilege and duty of the gathered church, we will be eager to spend a significant portion of our corporate worship doing it together.

Third, our substantial prayer together with the church in corporate worship should be *elder-led*. By this I mean that it is the duty primarily of the elders of the church[6]—the under-shepherds of Christ's flock—to be the voice of the congregation in prayer. To be clear: prayer is the right of every man, woman, or child who belongs to Christ. An elder in the church has no greater standing before God in prayer than the weakest or youngest believer. He will not be answered more readily or more lovingly than any other child of the King. Neither is an elder the church's mediator. His prayers do not secure the attention of the Father; we have only one Mediator—equally advocating for all the redeemed—the man Christ Jesus (1 Tim. 2:15). Instead, the elder is the servant leader of the congregation. He goes ahead of them, giving voice to their prayers, and he comes alongside them, encouraging them to join their hearts to the common petition.

Throughout redemptive history, the leaders of God's people have always had the privileged responsibility of praying publicly. Moses, Joshua, Samuel, David, Hezekiah, Nehemiah, Ezra, and Daniel each prayed as the voice of the covenant community and stand as examples for today's church leaders. Furthermore, just as it was given to the apostles to focus their efforts on "prayer and . . . the ministry of the word" (Acts 6:4), and just as nonapostolic pastors such as Timothy and Epaphras later prioritized these same functions to serve the first-century church, so it is the special task of our own elders to lead the local church in prayer.[7]

By *elder-led*, I also mean that the elders generally should not read written prayers but should lead in their own words. Historically, extemporaneous prayer in corporate worship was typical across a variety of Protestant traditions, including Presbyterian, Congregational, Baptist, and Methodist churches.[8] Such "free" prayer, still valued in many churches today, gets its rationale from the diverse prayers we see in Scripture, from the universal practice of the church for several hundred years after Christ and also following the Reformation, and from the conviction that only free prayer can adequately address the various specific needs and circumstances of a church.[9] Praying free prayers full of scriptural language, shaped by scriptural priorities, and based on scriptural promises best allows the elders to tenderly love and disciple the particular church under their care.[10]

In their letter to the Thessalonian church, Paul, Silvanus, and Timothy report: "We give thanks to God always for all of you, constantly mentioning you in our prayers, remembering before our God and Father your work of faith and labor of love and steadfastness of hope in our Lord Jesus Christ" (1 Thess. 1:2–3). In this same way, the elders in my own church intimately mention us before the Lord. Every week, they confess our common sins, remember our specific sufferings, ask for the fulfillment of our needs, and plead for our increased holiness. Often they pray for people and situations by name; always they pray with brotherly affection for all of us. They lead us in the hard work of prayer, not for their own personal good, but out of love. And praying alongside them, the gathered church receives training in the whole life of faith—growing in knowledge of God and of self, increasing in faith, and learning from these mature brothers how to pray.

Brothers and sisters, we must have substantial, elder-led prayer in corporate worship.

How to Pray While Someone Else Leads

Since infancy, I have sat weekly in the pews alongside my church and have been led in prayer together with them. I know this is a great privilege, and so I would love to be able to say that my heart has engaged every time. But it wouldn't be true. As a child, I squirmed and daydreamed through many prayers. As a teenager, I slept through a handful. And even as an adult, I find my mind sometimes distracted from the glorious purpose of our heavenly errand. Sadly, not every prayer has found me at the throne with everyone else.

How then should we pray while someone else leads? As I learned from those Highlanders on their feet, the key is recognizing that we must actually pray, and that we pray, in the quaint words of one writer, "every whit as heartily as [the] leader."[11] Corporate prayer is work for the whole church.

First, as obvious as it may sound, we must be present. We need to be present physically, "not neglecting to meet together" (Heb. 10:25). If we are not at the meetings of the church, we miss the opportunity to pray together. Also, we must be present mentally, paying attention to the petitions of the one who leads. Most importantly, we must be present spiritually, entering wholeheartedly into the common prayer because "uniting with others, in the most earnest petitions, where your own heart is unmoved, will avail you nothing."[12]

Second, having shown up, we make it our aim to say, "Amen." More than just a token ending to a prayer, "Amen" is our emphatic agreement and earnest hope that the God who hears prayer will grant our united request. In this spirit, the psalmist urges, "Let all the people say, 'Amen!'" (Ps. 106:48), and the apostle Paul directs Christians to pray clearly so that others can say, "Amen" (1 Cor. 14:16). Jesus, too, elevates agreement as our chief goal when we pray with others (Matt. 18:19).[13]

Keeping this focus promotes an attitude of humility and sub-mission. We are not there to criticize (or to praise) the quality of the prayer; we are there to seek whatever is biblical in it and to add our assent. Even the most imperfect, stumbling prayers often contain truth about God and his purposes that we can "Amen." We also seek whatever application we can make to our particular circumstances. Is the leader confessing the sin of idolatry? We examine our own hearts and repent of the instances we find. Is the leader praying for wisdom? We offer up to God the situations in which we find ourselves lacking discernment. In this way, the words of one person become "the joint and humble supplication of hundreds of penitent and believing souls, all engaged in pouring out their hearts to the God of salvation."[14] And all God's people said, "Amen."

Of course, we cannot do any of this in our own strength. Call-ing on the promised help of the Spirit (Rom. 8:26), we should pray before praying, pray about praying, and pray while praying. Like the familiar illustration of the duck—that glides serenely on the water's surface but is paddling frantically underneath—the members of the church may appear passive when praying to-gether, but in the invisible places we are each working very hard indeed.

Regular, Public Prayer Meetings in Church Life

Some of the most satisfying moments of my life have been spent doing projects with my local church. As a child I loved to help at church workdays, fetching hammers and cleaning paintbrushes for the adults. As a teenager I stood in the autumn air with other teens, raking leaves on the lawns of widows. As an adult I have traveled with church members, repairing a hurricane-damaged house, a tor-nado-wrecked Christian camp, and a timeworn residential school for young adults. Each time, when we were done, we workers gave one another sweaty high-fives and weary smiles. Well done.

I have sometimes thought we should do that at our Wednesday

night church prayer meeting. After an hour of prayer—an hour of hard work, of God glorified and neighbors helped, of significant things attempted for Christ and his kingdom—we could high-five one another with tears in our eyes. Well done. With the myriad of projects that church members find themselves doing together,[15] surely none is more important than the spiritual task that upholds every good work. We need *regular, public prayer meetings in church life.*

In an earlier century, I might not have had to define what I mean by *prayer meeting.* Once a common practice, the "general prayer meeting" or "social prayer meeting"[16] has sadly disappeared in many modern-day churches. The prayer meeting is a gathering of the local church for the purpose of praying together and with opportunity for those present to lead in prayer. The meeting might include Scripture reading, singing, or time for people to suggest items for prayer, but its focus—and the bulk of its time—is praying. Typically, this will mean that one member after another takes a brief turn leading the others in prayer together.

In the first place, our prayer meetings have an important place *in church life.* As we saw in chapters 4 and 5, praying together is an excellent way for God's people to grow in love for one another and to disciple one another in holiness. "There are many parts, yet one body" (1 Cor. 12:20), and this is beautifully expressed in a church prayer meeting. The thanksgiving of one person reminds another of a related blessing; the praise of one is expanded by another; and the request of one is taken up and advanced by someone else. We pray for one another and we pray with one another, allowing another's public prayers to give rise to our own. We are the body.

Second, our prayer meetings should be *regular.* A regular church prayer meeting affirms the importance of prayer. The church simply has too much work to do not to pray. She is given the enormous task of worshiping God, loving his people, doing good, and proclaiming Christ in the world. But without a regular prayer meeting, the church might only feel the necessity of praying together in the face of an impending crisis—or, worse, never. With a regular prayer meeting, the church acknowledges her moment-by-moment dependence on her God. The prayer meeting is also an important way for God's people to remember kingdom concerns outside of the local body—pleading with God for the success of missions, the deliverance of the persecuted, and the establishment of the church everywhere. Finally, a regular prayer meeting gives church members frequent opportunities to lead in prayer, allowing each one to gain confidence and facility in praying publicly.

Third, our church prayer meetings should be *public*. By this I mean that the prayer meeting should be an official meeting of the church, open to everyone who can attend. There is certainly a valuable place for praying with discipleship groups, ministry teams, Sunday school classes, or friends (and I will discuss those in the next chapter), but the church is bigger than any one group, and her prayer together should reflect this.[17] We meet to pray together as a colony of heaven: a diverse community of ages, genders, ethnicities, and gifts. The benefits of this were poignantly defended in one 1835 handbook for church members:

> It [the prayer meeting] tends to keep alive the spirit of devotion—demonstrates, by the prayers of so many brethren who engage, the minor varieties, yet prevailing uniformity, of [C]hristian experience,—humbles the rich by the holy gifts and graces of the poor—encourages the poor by the sympathies, confessions, and acknowledgements of the rich—cheers the heart of the minister by the kind interest and fervent supplications of his flock—cements the minds of the members,—and may be supposed to bring down the blessings of God upon the church, which is thus united in supplication, and also upon all those varied objects which the church bears before God in believing prayer.[18]

Brothers and sisters, we need regular, public prayer meetings in our church life.

How to Lead While Others Pray

If the fear of public speaking is the general population's greatest fear, fear of praying publicly may be its Christian equivalent. It is no wonder. In prayer together, the leader brings his brothers and sisters on a holy errand to the very throne room of almighty God. But the fear of the Lord is the beginning of knowledge (Prov. 1:7), and appreciating the enormity of the task can lead us to appreciate the enormity of our help. As we noted in chapter 1, the Christian never prays alone. And the Christian never leads others in prayer by himself but always has the promised and sufficient help of the three: the listening Father, the mediating and interceding Son, and the helping Spirit.

With this confidence, you can take steps (I'll suggest three) to better lead others in prayer. First, be ready. This has several aspects. Your readiness for public prayer always begins with a regular habit of private prayer. As Samuel Miller wrote in *Thoughts on Public Prayer*, "None can hope to attain excellence in the grace and gift of prayer in the public assembly, unless they abound in closet devotion, and in holy communion with God in secret."[19] You also get ready by studying the prayers in Scripture and by paying attention to the public prayers of more mature believers. Too, you get ready to pray publicly by thinking ahead about what you might pray. Maybe a verse from your private Scripture reading or the application from a recent sermon, maybe a particular mission field or gospel opportunity, maybe a suffering friend or struggling church could become the subject of your prayer. Beyond that, you get ready to pray by resolving that you will pray if given opportunity. If you don't intend to pray, you likely never will.

Second, be clear. Your great aim as you lead others in prayer is that they would pray along with you. Jesus strongly warns against thoughtless rambling (Matt. 6:7) and hypocrisy and pride (Matt. 6:5). Instead, you should pray with simplicity and humility, encouraging others to join their hearts to yours. It is good to pick one or two items for prayer and pray thoroughly and briefly about them; this allows others to "Amen" your petitions and leaves time for others to lead. The words and sentences of your prayer should also be clear; use the language of Scripture informed by your natural way of speaking.

Third, be corporate. When you lead in public prayer, you are not praying for yourself only but also with others. You are asking them to join you as you approach God and to make your petitions their own. For this reason, you should try as much as possible to use corporate language ("we," "us," and "our") and to pray for things that are common to everyone.

On a recent Wednesday night, my six-year-old son prayed aloud in the church prayer meeting. He prayed for missionaries to preach the gospel, for Muslims to trust in Christ for their salvation, and for the sick people in our congregation to get better. His prayer was sincere, simply expressed, and very brief. It was just what the church needed. Brothers and sisters, your most feeble prayer may unite the hearts of the church before God. By the help of the Spirit, you may remind them of forgotten truth, stir them to renewed desire, or move them to greater love. At the very least, your prayer will cause them to pray together. And that is just what they need.

The Truth We Tell

Martyn Lloyd-Jones wrote, "There is nothing that tells the truth about us as a Christian people so much as our prayer life,"[20] meaning that our practice of the demanding, countercultural, invisible, and uncomfortable work of prayer is an excellent test of our attitude toward the God who calls us to it. The same could be said for churches. The local church tells the truth about her corporate spiritual condition by her practice of prayer together.

Brothers and sisters, do you pray with the church?

8

Praying with Partners
and Groups

In a campus dorm, two college roommates bow their heads in prayer together as they have done every night for a semester. In a suburban living room, neighbors meet weekly to pray for their neighborhood and city. In an auditorium, hundreds of Christians from several area churches unite in an evening of prayer for revival. In an office building, coworkers arrive early to ask the Lord for grace for their workday. On the steps of the town hall, citizens assemble to give thanks to God and to intercede for their nation. In an elementary school basement, mothers pray twice a month for the students and staff. In a book-filled study, three pastors pray for one another and for the churches under their care. In a church building, local Christians gather on Sunday afternoons to intercede for the persecuted church throughout the world. At a restaurant table, four friends pray urgently about the cancer diagnosis one has just received.

These examples are not imaginary. Each happened—some are happening right now—in my life or in my community. Nor are these examples exhaustive. I could add, and I am sure you could add, many more. Childhood friends pray together regularly on the phone, discipleship groups spend part of their meetings in prayer, and communities shaken by tragedy gather for late-night prayer services. Our opportunities for praying with partners and groups are diverse. Some prayer is the activity of a specific, committed group of people. Some prayer is open to anyone who wants to attend. Some prayer is carefully planned, marked on the calendar and focused on particular concerns. Some prayer is spontaneous, compelled in the moment by a sudden need or a cause for rejoicing. Some prayer is an annual—or even a one-time—event. Some prayer is frequent and regular, occurring faithfully every Tuesday or Saturday or first Monday. At all times, in all places, among all kinds of people, Christians are praying together.

Earlier, I quoted Dietrich Bonhoeffer: "It is in fact the most normal thing in the common Christian life to pray together."[1] Has this been your experience? It is my goal in this chapter to encourage praying together in our ordinary, daily lives. I hope we can make praying with our friends and in our communities a normal part of our Christian experience. To this end, we will consider three important elements of praying with partners and groups—who, what, when (and where)—and discover new opportunities to pray together.

Who: Finding a Community of Prayer

We noted in chapter 1 that our relationship to Christ brings us into relationship with everyone else who is united to him. We are branches on the same vine (John 15:5), stones in the same building (1 Pet. 2:5), and parts of the same body (1 Cor. 12:12).We were together made alive, together raised up, and together seated in heaven (Eph. 2:4–7). It is right, therefore, that our earthly relationships should also manifest our shared spiritual life. People who live or work together have common trials and common joys. Christians who live or work together can take those things to God in prayer. In all the spheres of our life—with our Christian neighbors, coworkers, classmates, teammates, church group members, and friends[2]—we have reason to pray together.

Praying together also allows Christians to affirm our unity in Christ even when we may hold diverse convictions. Describing the prayer meetings of 1858, Samuel Prime wrote:

> Christians of both sexes, of all ages, of different denominations, without the slightest regard to denominational distinctions, came together, on one common platform of brotherhood in Christ, and in the bonds of Christian union sent up their united petitions to the throne of the heavenly giver. The question was never asked, "To what church does he belong?" But the question was, "Does he belong to Christ?"[3]

This simple question ought to be our question too. We can pray with anyone and everyone who knows the listening Father, who trusts in the mediating Son, and who has received the helping Spirit.[4] Though classmates or coworkers may interpret particular Scripture passages differently, though we may disagree on certain theological and doctrinal principles, though we may each join churches with variations in worship and government, all who belong to Christ can pray together.

Earlier this year, nine churches in my community joined together for a prayer meeting. Baptists, Pentecostals, and Presbyterians bowed their heads side by side, united in prayer, asking for the glory of God and for the outpouring of his Spirit in our city. Our sincere theological differences probably will not be resolved on this side of heaven. But our common life, our common needs, and our common Savior bring us together before our God.

If it is good for us to pray in all our human relationships, it is especially sweet to pray regularly with our closest friends. As Proverbs tells us: "A friend loves at all times, and a brother is born for adversity" (Prov. 17:17). Our friends eagerly share the full range of our human experiences. They rejoice at our blessings. They weep at our losses. They listen to our stories. They tell us their stories in return. With our friends, we reveal our frailties, sins, desires, and hopes. How fitting then that we would also take all those things together to the Lord! Like the prayers of Daniel and his three companions (Dan. 2:17–18), or of Paul and his friend Silas (Acts 16:25), our praying together is an important part of true friendship.

One summer I returned home from college feeling unexpectedly depressed. Without classmates or schoolwork I was listless and aimless, and the long days alone while my parents were at work just reinforced my sense of displacement. And then Sharon called. She invited me to do two things: to walk four miles with her every morning and to pray together as we walked. Sharon was a friend; we had lived on the same street and worshiped at the same church for years. That summer she proved to be my sister for adversity. In my lowest moments, side by side and day by day, we walked, we talked, and especially we prayed. Since that time, I have walked and prayed in other neighborhoods with other friends, and each time we have found our friendship sweetened by together bringing our sorrows and joys to that mutual Friend who always prays for us both.

Brothers and sisters, with whom could you pray?

What: Identifying a Focus of Prayer

Last week, I attended our church small group in a member's living room. As everyone arrived, we arranged ourselves in a circle: on chairs, couches, benches, and even on the floor. After a few minutes, the leader began the meeting by asking, "Okay, what items do we have for prayer?" People uncapped their pens and jotted notes on the back of the week's study sheet as various members gave requests. Then we prayed about them together.

I'm sure this is a familiar scenario to many of us. We typically begin our prayer times by identifying what we are going to pray about. This is good. Prayer is an activity with content—"an offering up of our desires"[5]—and we must recognize something we want before we can ask for it. Especially in a group, where our goal is unified prayer from every heart, advance direction is particularly helpful. Here we will look at three approaches: choosing a single topic, praying systematically through items on a list, or taking requests from every person. These formats are not mutually exclusive—I have been in many prayer meetings that allot time to all three—but each has value as we cast our burdens on the Lord together.

First, we can choose in advance a single focus for praying together. This allows us to develop that topic more fully in prayer and to together invest our hearts more deeply in the cause. In selecting our topic, we must always remember that God himself sets the priorities for our prayers. We come to the hallowed one—the kingdom establisher, the bread giver, the sin forgiver, the Satan defeater (Matt. 6:9–13)—asking him to do those things he delights to do. Under this framework we can identify a particular need, often a burden that we naturally share with those with whom we pray. For example, we might choose to dedicate ourselves to praying together for:

- churches to be planted in a specific place,
- a particular person to come to Christ and be saved,
- a sick Christian brother or sister to be healed,
- certain pervasive sins in our community to be confessed and forsaken,
- or our persecuted brothers and sisters to be vindicated.[6]

Second, we can pray together in a systematic way for the whole number of gospel opportunities, churches, and individuals. Throughout the New Testament Epistles, the apostles and the churches deliberately and constantly "remember" one another in prayer (Eph. 1:16; Col. 4:18; 1 Thess. 1:2–3; 2 Tim. 1:3; Phil. 1:4; Philem. 4; Heb. 13:3). But, sadly, we often forget to pray for certain things, allowing the more urgent or more familiar situations to dominate our prayer time. In order to remember, we can use directories or lists to pray together for each of the:

- members of our local church;
- residents, employees, students, or volunteers in the places we live or work;
- churches in our community or in our denomination;
- civil authorities over our city, county, state, and nation;
- missionaries supported by our local church or working for a particular organization;
- nations of the world and the church in those nations.[7]

Finally, we can pray together for the personal requests of group members. As we noted in chapter 4, praying together for one another—bearing one another's burdens and rejoicing in their blessings—produces the fruit of mutual love. And in order to pray for one another, we have to know their needs. Recently I had a conversation with a woman who was reluctant to ask her Bible study group to pray about a significant concern in her life. "Every time we take requests," she told me, "I almost start to say something. But then I don't. Maybe I will next week." As uncomfortable or humbled or exposed as we might sometimes feel about sharing our prayer needs, we can remember that our requests will allow others to bring us before the throne and that our relationships with them will deepen as a result. The apostle Paul himself frequently included personal prayer requests in his letters: that he would be given gospel opportunities (Col. 4:3), that he could visit the Thessalonian believers (1 Thess. 3:10), that his ministry would have success (2 Thess. 3:1), and that he could see his friend Philemon (Philem. 22). If Paul did not hesitate to ask for prayer, we should not either.

Sometimes, however, our prayer requests go astray. The request time wanders into gossip about church members. Parents use prayer as an excuse to reveal their children's private sins. Spouses use it to complain about one another. Some requests are inscrutably vague while others contain too much detail. Trials become grumblings. Blessings become boasts.

Before sharing a request, we should ask ourselves:

- Is this request something I could expect God to grant? Do I have biblical reason to think my desire is according to God's revealed will? Can I ask other people to add their "Amen" to this request?

- Is this request appropriate for everyone present to know? Do I expose someone else's private sins or concerns by sharing this request? Will this request encourage genuine love for God and for neighbor?

In turn, we should receive the genuine concerns of others with love. Sinners saved by grace have no room for self-righteousness. And even imperfect or immature requests are our opportunity to bear the burdens of Christ's brothers and sisters. Let us not be like the disciples who thought the needs of little children were too trifling for Jesus's prayer. Let us be like Jesus who lived according to the eternal kingdom and eagerly prayed for its weakest members (Matt. 19:13–15).

Whether we are praying together with a specific focus, a systematic plan, or according to the requests of others, our task seems enormous. We can never pray together for everything. The vast number of items for prayer can quickly overwhelm a single pair of friends or a small handful of coworkers, briefly bowing their heads on a Friday morning. Brothers and sisters, take heart! Our prayers are just one precious drop in that heavenly bowl that contains all the prayers of God's people from Adam until now (Rev. 5:8). Our prayers are just one note in that divine groan that the Spirit utters before the Father (Rom. 8:26). And our prayers are just one "Amen" to that perfect petition that the Son never stops praying on our behalf (Heb. 7:25). Our own prayer lists always fall short, but the requests before the throne never do.

Brothers and sisters, despite our weaknesses and failings, before the Father, by the help of the Spirit and through the blood of the Son, each request we pray together is God's means for accomplishing his perfect purpose in the world.

When and Where: Fostering a Culture of Prayer

On August 22, 1727, in present-day Germany, members of the Moravian Church determined "that it might be well to set apart certain hours for the purpose of prayer, at which seasons all might be reminded of its excellency and be induced by the promise annexed to fervent, persevering prayer, to pour out their hearts before the Lord."[8] They proceeded to organize a twenty-four-hour prayer vigil with men and women volunteering to pray during each hour of the day. It continued for the next hundred years.

As its organizers had hoped, the "Hourly Intercession" established a priority of prayer for the whole community. In addition to the hourly prayers, every evening each church member met with an assigned partner for prayer.[9] Friends were encouraged to "live in the habit of close familiarity, join in prayer, and act, in all respects as intimate friendship requires."[10] And, regularly, the congregation held special days of prayer, either to give thanks together on the anniversary of a blessing or to intercede together for a specific need.[11] Hour by hour and day by day, in homes, fields, and meeting rooms, the people prayed together.

We, too, can nurture a culture of praying together by practicing both scheduled prayer and spontaneous prayer. First, we need regularly scheduled prayer. The Moravians made prayer an intentional part of their days, the early church gathered for prayer "day by day" (Acts 2:46), and we too must designate time for prayer. Whether it is every morning on the phone with a friend or every third Thursday at the park with neighborhood moms, regular prayer together reminds us of its necessity and disciplines us by its faithful practice. In a culture enamored of spontaneity and so-called authenticity, it is important for us to realize that we must first form the *habit* of praying together before we will instinctively pray together in all the little moments of our days.[12]

Second, we need to pray together spontaneously. Praying together should become something not just for one day a week but for every day, not only for inside the church building but outside it too. We should say to one another not just, "Would you remember to pray for me?" but, "Would you pray with me right now?" Not, "I'll pray about that," but, "Let's pray about that together." Praying together should be a way of life.

Watch and Pray

A friend once told me that when she was on the mission field, she prayed every morning for "divine appointments"—for the Lord to bring gospel-hungry people into her path. Then she set herself to the tasks of the day looking for the Lord's answer. Invariably, she had conversations with people whom she might otherwise have ignored, and she deliberately spoke of Christ to them. Her daily prayer had two results: the Lord gave opportunities, and he opened her eyes to see them.

What if we prayed for "prayer appointments"? What if we looked daily for God-given moments to pray together? By prayer and expectation we may discover that a friendship, a crisis, a Bible study meeting, a phone call, or a hospital room reveals yet another occasion to gather at the throne.

Brothers and sisters, "Watch for favorable opportunities of prayer."[13]

9

Praying with Family
and Guests

My husband's grandmother smiled to see us even as she worked to coax words into sense. She was ninety-three years old, gripping her chair with feeble fingers and her memories with a failing mind. "God has," she began. We nodded encouragingly in the silence until she said, "God has . . . done . . . so many things." She sighed with the effort and the relief at having said something we understood. A minute later she tried another sentence: "My parents." Then, a long pause as she gathered herself. "We . . . prayed . . . each day."

Grandma's parents may have seemed unremarkable in this world, but they were regularly granted an audience in heaven. And their daughter remembered those frequent family prayers for nearly one hundred years. From her praying childhood, she grew up to pray with her own husband and children. Those seven children then prayed with their families, and, in one of them, my husband first learned to call on the name of the Lord. Now he and I pray together, and our children make the fifth generation to daily offer their desires before the throne. The practice of one household has become the priority of many.

This chapter will encourage praying together in our homes. Of course, many of the things we considered in the last chapter about praying with partners and groups apply to praying in the home. A spouse makes a natural prayer partner; a family with children forms a natural prayer group. If we pray with friends and coworkers, we should pray all the more with the people in our homes. In our homes, our hair down and our shoes off, we inevitably practice the true priorities of our hearts. Praying together ought to be one of them. To this end, we will discuss praying with family members, particularly our spouses and children. Then we will discuss praying with guests as an act of hospitality and as an element of evangelism.

Brothers and sisters, marriages and meals are made holy by prayer (1 Tim. 4:1–5).

Praying with Your Spouse

"If there were but two human beings upon the earth, they would be drawn, if they were of sanctified hearts, to pray with one another."[1] With these words, nineteenth-century minister and theologian J. W. Alexander anchored his case for regular worship in the home. As people in relationship to one another and to our triune God, as people bound by God's commands and compelled by his promises, we are drawn to pray.[2] A man and a woman, purchased by Christ's blood and joined in marriage, should talk together to their God.

When we consider the Bible's teaching on marriage, it is no surprise that praying regularly with our spouse is assumed. Peter gives this direction: "Likewise, husbands, live with your wives in an understanding way, showing honor to the woman as the weaker vessel, since they are heirs with you of the grace of life, so that your prayers may not be hindered" (1 Pet. 3:7). Seventeenth-century theologian Robert Leighton commented on this verse:

He [Peter] supposes in Christians the necessary and frequent use of this; takes it for granted, that the heirs of life cannot live without prayer. This is the proper breathing and language of these heirs. . . . These heirs, if they be alone, they pray alone; if heirs together, and living together, they pray together. [3]

In Peter's instructions, we see that praying together is the normal practice of a marriage lived "in God's sight" (1 Pet. 3:4; cf. 3:12). As Christian husbands and wives, we rejoice at one another's successes, we consider one another's needs, and we bear with one another's sins so that we might bring those things before our Lord in prayer. Our love for one another and for our God will express itself in prayer together, and, as we pray together, we will inevitably love each other better.[4]

But if your marriage is anything like mine, time is of the essence. Most couples have lists and calendars and scheduled alerts jammed with responsibilities: trash pickup, Bible study, grocery shopping, dentist appointment, carpool, soccer practice, business trip. Just running a household requires more energy than most marriages can find, and praying together often takes its cobwebbed place on the list of Things to Do Later. In the whirlwind of life, when are we going to pray? And is it really all that important anyway?

This is not a modern problem. People have always allowed eating, drinking, and dressing to consume more attention than they ought (Matt. 6:25–31) and to push spiritual duties to the slender margins. Like many of us, the members of the first-century church also found themselves confused about their marital priorities. And the Lord, through the apostle Paul, clarifies for everyone: "Do not deprive one another, except perhaps by agreement for a limited time, that you may devote yourselves to prayer" (1 Cor. 7:5). First, he affirms the value of physical intimacy in marriage: "Do not deprive one another." While playfulness and pleasure might seem optional in a busy married life, in God's good design they are actually essential. *Do not* deprive one another. But as important as sexual intimacy is, the Lord allows one thing to occasionally eclipse it: "except . . . that you may devote yourselves to prayer." Praying together is so vital for married couples that if time and energy are in short supply, all other obligations should move down on the to-do list.[5]

The Westminster Confession of Faith rightly exhorts us to worship God "in private families daily."[6] If you and your spouse are early risers, pray together when you first wake up. If you tend to watch TV or work on projects far into the night, pray together before going to bed. If you share a meal, a ride to work, or a late-afternoon phone call every day, make one of those an occasion for prayer. And if you have children in the home and already pray together with them daily, you might choose to set a separate time once a week to pray exclusively with your spouse. Too, as needs or decisions arise—and they do in every marriage—make spontaneous prayer together your first response. Amid the cares and riches and pleasures of life, husbands and wives practice together the priorities of heaven, of which we are fellow heirs.

Praying with Your Children

Karis is a five-year-old girl in my church. She has Krabbe disease, which progressively destroys the myelin in her nerve cells, and she cannot walk or talk. She also has a soul that will never die.[7] It is difficult to know how much Karis understands, but her brown eyes widen for anyone privileged enough to sit beside her wheelchair and speak to her. Every day her parents pray with her. They pray for her healing with greater urgency than most of us have ever felt, but Karis's physical well-being is not the end of their prayers together. They pray too for her soul and for their own. Then they pull out the church prayer list, and, item by item, Karis and her parents remember the needs of the saints before their heavenly Father. In eternity, the many will give thanks for their prayers.

As Christian parents, our first responsibility to our children is to pray *in front of them* and *on their behalf*. Our children need to hear us pray, and they need to hear us pray for them, bringing them before our God. When Jesus the God-man was on the earth, parents also carried their children to him: "Then children were brought to him that he might lay his hands on them and pray. The disciples rebuked the people, but Jesus said, 'Let the little children come to me and do not hinder them, for to such belongs the kingdom of heaven.' And he laid his hands on them and went away" (Matt. 19:13–15). Sadly, we have often mentally reduced this scene to a serene storybook illustration: smiling moms and dads posing their kids for a celebrity photo with Jesus. These children weren't physically sick, and so we might think the parents were requesting a nice ritual—a symbolic gesture of Jesus's love for kids in general. Not so.

Brothers and sisters, those parents must have been desperate.[8] While some brought their children to Jesus, many did not. We must appreciate that the parents who asked Jesus to pray for their kids were just as determined as the friends of the paralytic clawing their way through the roof (Luke 5:17–26), or as the man with a demon-possessed son who *begged* Jesus to free his child (Luke 9:37–43). Those moms and dads were not coming to Jesus and defying the irate disciples for a souvenir. They were rushing the priceless souls of their dead-in-sin children to the only hospital with a cure.

When each of our sons was baptized, my husband and I vowed "to pray with and for him."[9] This is no incidental task. It is not merely a sweet-dreams prayer at a toddler's bedside or a brief thanks at the table before the food gets cold—though it is at least those. Praying "with and for" our children is interceding in their hearing for their salvation. It is inconveniencing ourselves so our children might meet the Savior of sinners. It is faith and persistence in the face of every obstacle. It is loudly begging Christ to do for their souls what we cannot. It is bringing them to Jesus so *he* might pray for them. Like the importunity of the parents in Matthew 19, it is desperation.

And experiencing this will always impress our children's souls.

As Terry Johnson writes, "Our children should grow up with the voices of their fathers pleading for their souls in prayer ringing in their ears, leading to their salvation, or else haunting them for the rest of their lives."[10] Morning by morning, evening by evening, at the breakfast table, or in the car, or as they snuggle into bed, our children must hear us praying urgently for them.

It is not enough, however, simply to pray *in front of* our children and *on behalf of* our children. We also have a duty to *teach our children to pray for themselves*. Before God's throne, the prayers of believing children are welcome—even essential. Jesus made this point, using the words of Psalm 8, at the time of his Triumphal Entry:

> But when the chief priests and the scribes saw the wonderful things that he [Jesus] did, and the children crying out in the temple, "Hosanna to the Son of David!" they were indignant, and they said to him, "Do you hear what these are saying?" And Jesus said to them, "Yes; have you never read, 'Out of the mouth of infants and nursing babies you have prepared praise'?" (Matt. 21:15–16)

Not only does Jesus hear what little children say in prayer; he has ordained their praises from all eternity. Your childhood prayers and mine, and each of the prayers of your children and my children and of the generations yet to be born (Ps. 102:12, 18) are a rebuke to God's enemies and a public testimony of God's glory.

One of the best ways we can encourage our children to pray is to teach them during daily times of family prayer. As we saw in chapter 5, much of what we ourselves know about praying comes from listening to others pray. When parents pray aloud with their children, the little ones are learning—even unconsciously—the patterns, priorities, language, and attitude of prayer. But young children will also benefit from direct instruction in how to pray. In his day, Jonathan Edwards staunchly defended the right of children to pray, even if their heartfelt prayers were sometimes nonsensical to adults. However, he wrote, "'Tis fit that care should be taken of them [children], by their parents and pastors, to instruct and direct them, and to correct imprudent conduct and irregularities, if they are perceived."[11]

As soon as our children could speak, my husband and I found it helpful to lead them in prayer, whispering into their ears one phrase or sentence at a time for them to repeat to the Lord. Eventually, we asked them to suggest their own praises and petitions, which we then put into words for them. Finally, they began to pray independently, guided by the list of praises, thanksgivings, confessions, and supplications we discuss beforehand.[12] In this way, it is my daily privilege to be led to the heavenly Jerusalem by the hosannas of children.

We have great reason to hope that God will answer our prayers with and for our children by granting them saving faith (Acts 2:39). And the practice of regularly—daily!—praying with them has immense value:[13]

- It demonstrates for children that prayer is vital.
- It trains children in theology, in godly reason, and in piety.
- It reminds parents that their children have souls.
- It affirms the fundamental, equal spiritual identity of both parents and children as the children of a heavenly Father.
- It unites families in longsuffering and mutual love as they confess their sins together.[14]
- It humbles both parents and children with the acknowledgment that they cannot meet their own needs.
- It comforts families in the midst of grief and trial.
- It orients families in the midst of blessing and joy.
- It disciplines both parents and children in the regular habit of prayer.
- It reinforces and proclaims the spiritual priorities of a Christian home.

Brothers and sisters, let us bring our children to Jesus.

Praying with Your Guests

A Hindu and a Christian walked into our house. These men were not the first line of a joke but new friends—students from India now living nearby. We invited them to dinner. We ate chicken biryani together and exchanged stories of family, and travel, and curry so hot you can't breathe. We also prayed. We prayed before the meal, thanking our Lord, the giver of daily bread, and we prayed during our regular time of family worship after the meal. They were in our house for only a few hours, but they left knowing our love for them and, more importantly, our love for our Lord.

We have already discussed how we ought to pray with our spouses and our children. Now we will consider how that practice extends to our guests. Whether we are welcoming friends for coffee or hosting them for a weekend, our prayers together refresh the hearts of saints and stand as a testimony to the unconverted.

When our guests are fellow Christians, praying together ought to be an element of the hospitality that God repeatedly commands us to offer (Rom. 12:13; Heb. 13:2; 1 Pet. 4:9). As Alexander writes, "We are, perhaps, ready enough to make our guests welcome, to provide for their lodging and refreshment, to show them the wonders of our environs, and to invite friends for their entertainment; but, besides this, we owe a duty to their souls."[15] For our guests, praying together provides a home away from home. They are not able to pray with their own families, so we invite them to pray with ours. Conversely, nothing could be less welcoming than sharing with guests the physical provisions of our home while thoughtlessly excluding them from its source of spiritual nourishment!

Praying before mealtimes is probably the most obvious way to pray together with guests. It was certainly the practice of the early church who "received their food with glad and generous hearts" (Acts 2:46), and we shouldn't neglect it either. Every time we break bread we thank its giver, whoever our dinner companions are. Our prayers stand as an encouragement to believing guests and a living sermon to unbelieving ones. Jesus prayed before his post-resurrection meal with two of his disciples (Luke 24:30), and Paul prayed before his shipboard meal with two hundred pagan sailors (Acts 27:35–37). When the church in Acts devoted themselves to eating and praying together, "the Lord added to their number day by day those who were being saved" (Acts 2:47). Who knows what impact our sincere acknowledgment of God will have on those with whom we share a meal?

We also ought to invite guests to our regular times of family prayer. This is a unique opportunity for gospel witness to unbelievers. Often in our evangelistic conversations with non-Christians the terms of our discussion are dictated by them: "Do you really think homosexuality is a sin?" "What about abortion?" "Are you against birth control?" "What do you think about evolution, climate change, and the church's view of women?" Each of these presents valid issues to which the Scripture has substantive answers. But none of them is *the* issue: the responsibility of every human being to submit to the triune Lord. In our homes and at prayer, we have the unique freedom to set the terms of engagement, to focus our guests on the true priorities of a Christian's heart. Having nourished our friends' bodies, we offer them bread for their soul. As we pray, we proclaim to our guests—and remind ourselves!—that we are each spiritual beings who owe worship to God and approach him only through the blood of Christ. Just as the prayers of Stephen doubtless rang in the ears of Saul (Acts 7:58–60; 22:20), and then the prayers of Saul—now Paul—doubtless rang in the ears of the jailer at Philippi (Acts 16:25, 30), the testimony of our family prayers may lead to the salvation of many. We may one day find our past dinner guests seated beside us at the great wedding feast of the Lamb.

Brothers and sisters—without hesitation or apology, for the good of our families and guests, in obedience to the Word, for the glory of our God—let us pray together in our homes.

Conclusion

In the chapters you just read, I told a lot of stories.

There's the story about the Praying Indians and the one about the praying bully. I told a story about the little woman who started a great revival and one about a bunch of kids who taught the grown-ups how to pray. I talked about the teenagers who prayed in the outhouse and about the country church that prayed on Wednesday nights. I even told a story or two about my own children.

You may have read these stories and thought I forgot a few. I didn't tell about George Müller and the prayers at his orphanage. I didn't tell about Amy Carmichael and the praying missionaries in India. I didn't tell about those students at Oxford University—George Whitefield and the Wesley brothers—who prayed together every morning at six o'clock. I didn't even mention the church prayer meeting at the Metropolitan Tabernacle under C. H. Spurgeon.

Those are great stories. But the ones I told were about praying saints you've likely never heard of. I did that on purpose. It's all too easy for us to read about the famous pray-ers and wrongly think of their prayer meetings as a different order of praying together. But you and your family, you and your friends, you and your church are just as much God's means for moving heaven and earth.

During the American Civil War one military hospital chaplain reported:

It would be sure to move your hearts if you could see those men come into our [prayer] meetings. Some come in on crutches, some on sticks and canes; some with bandages around their heads; some with broken arms, and some with broken legs; some blind, some sick—too sick to be out of bed, but creeping into the prayer-meetings because they are so anxious on the subject of religion that they cannot stay away.[1]

Brothers and sisters, we hobble to prayer meetings on crutches. We come painfully aware that our faith and our obedience and our prayers aren't what they should be. But as we advance slowly down the hallway, we see from every corridor the procession of the wounded, also coming to pray. We join their company, not because we are healthy but because we are sick, not because we are rich but because we are poor, not because we are powerful but because we know the One who is. We together stumble into the prayer meeting and find—joy of all joys!—that Christ himself is waiting for us there (Matt. 18:20).

Praying together is for you, my brother, my sister. You, suffering one, may be the next person to call friends to pray at your bedside and find that a revival breaks out. You, little one, may be a child in that long line of ordinary children whose prayers bring adults to their knees. You, dear church, may be in that company of praying men and women whose names disappear totally from the history books but who will be remembered forever in heaven.

Brothers and sisters, let us pray.

Acknowledgments

Thanks be to God

for Rob, heir with me of the grace of life, who sharpened my thinking with iron and warmed my heart with encouragement;

for my parents, Brad and Patsy Evans, who first taught me to pray, and for Carol Norman, who continued my education;

for my children, Brad, Caleb, and Nathan, whose little voices and big prayers lead me daily to the throne;

for Nathan Lee, Carol Hill, Rob, and Dad, who read draft upon draft and improved every one, and for Guy Waters, who batted cleanup;

for Melissa Kruger, without whose wise help and generous friendship the study questions could never have been written;

for Lindsey Carlson, who told me I was no J. I. Packer but who cheered me on anyway;

for Gloria Furman, Kathleen Neilson, and Collin Hansen, who offered me their personal encouragement and the support of The Gospel Coalition;

for Caryn Rivadeneira, Michelle Van Loon, and all the writers at Her.meneutics, who exhorted me to write a book on prayer and who were a community to me while I did so;

for the Women Who Write Stuff, who put one good sentence after another and remind me that writing stuff is kingdom work;

and for the multitude of Christ's brothers and sisters who helped me by prayer.

Study Questions

Introduction

Think back over times in your past when you have joined with others in prayer. Which of those times remains particularly memorable to you? Why? What fruits do you see in your own heart and life as a result of praying together?

Chapter 1: Relationship

Getting Started: If you were to go to a park and ask various individuals, "Why do people pray?" what type of responses do you think you'd get? If you were to go into a church and ask the same question, do you think you would hear similar answers?

1. What is the impact of viewing prayer as a relational conversation rather than as therapy for our problems or a Magic 8 Ball for our questions? What does it look like in practice for prayer to have a relational element?

2. Read Hebrews 10:19–22. What is the basis for our access to relationship with God? What changes us from enemies, strangers, and aliens to beloved children of God who can call upon God as "our Father" (Matt. 6:9)? What difference does it make when we believe that we are beloved children as we come to prayer?

3. In what way is God in relationship with himself? What is meant by the word *Trinity* as an explanation for God's nature?

4. Read Romans 8:14–34. What is the role of the Holy Spirit in our prayers? What is the role of the Father and of the Son?

5. How does the picture of Jesus as the vine and us as the branches (see John 15) provide a rich imagery of our interconnectedness as a church? What other examples are given in Scripture to describe the unity of the church as one entity with many parts? How does this concept affect and direct your prayers?

6. Read Revelation 8:3–4. What does this passage say our prayers look like from the perspective of heaven? How does this knowledge, that the prayers of the saints are all going to the same place, encourage us to pray together?

Further Study: Read Ephesians 1:3–14, a prayer of Paul.

- Nearly every verse in this prayer highlights an aspect of God's relationship with us. List the relational words and phrases you notice.

- How does Paul's prayer demonstrate understanding of God as Trinity? What does he say about the Father, the Son, and the Spirit? Do you pray with this same understanding?

- Paul's prayer repeatedly uses corporate language (*we, us, our*). How do you think this language would have affected the Ephesian believers who first read it? How does it affect you?

Chapter 2: Duty

Getting Started: What are some duties you have in your family, church, or community? In our day, people often think of duty as something joyless and oppressive. Why? What are some reasons to be thankful for the duties God places in your life?

1. What are some ways you notice corporate prayer being a natural part of Old Testament believers' relationship with God and with each other? What about corporate prayer among New Testament believers? How do we stand on their foundation today?

2. Read Daniel 2:1–24. What was Daniel's situation (vv. 1–16)? What was his immediate response (vv. 17–18)? After the Lord answered, what did the friends do (vv. 19–23)?

3. In Matthew 21:3 Jesus calls the temple a "house of prayer." Would you describe your church in that way? Your home? Is praying together a normal part of your relationship with others? Why or why not?

4. Turn back to page 37–38 and reread the different occasions of prayer in the book of Acts. What are some of the things the early Christians prayed for together? How do we pray these types of requests in the church today?

5. What opportunities do you have to pray with others? How can you be more intentional about making praying together a part of your daily life?

Further Study: Read Matthew 6:9–13, the Lord's Prayer.

- In Matthew 6:5 and 6:7, Jesus begins his instructions for prayer with "When you pray." How does this establish prayer as a duty?

- List the corporate phrases in this prayer (e.g., "our Father"). What does Jesus's corporate language teach us about our duty to pray together with others?

- What are the petitions (requests) in this prayer? How do we pray those things together in our churches, communities, and homes?

Chapter 3: Promise

Getting Started: How does the hope of blessing or reward spur you on in tasks that you find difficult?

1. What are some ways we are tempted to use a "mathematical notion of prayer" to force God to answer us? What is the problem with this approach?

2. Read Ephesians 6:10–20. What war are Christians fighting? How is praying together a part of our equipment? What characteristics should our prayer together have (vv. 18–19)? What is the guaranteed result?

3. In Psalm 34, David calls on the assembled people of God to praise the Lord together. What examples of corporate praise and thanksgiving can you think of in Scripture? In your own life? How does God use these praises?

4. What is the reference point for our agreement in prayer? Why is agreement so important? How does God promise to bless unified prayer?

5. When we pray for healing, what is the object of our faith? What two kinds of healing are described in James 5:13–16? Which do you tend to focus on when you pray with your family or church?

6. A non-Christian might assume that prayer is about getting our personal desires met. How might God's promises for praying together be surprising (or even disappointing) to a non-Christian or an immature Christian? How can we help one another to appreciate God's priorities as we pray together?

Further Study: Read Acts 4:23–31, the church's prayer for boldness.

- What are the believers asking God to do?

- What attributes and promises of God do they use to make their case in prayer? Why is this kind of arguing acceptable— and even welcome—before the throne?

- How do you think praying on the basis of God's revelation affected the believers' prayer together? How can God's promises give us confidence and expectation in prayer together today?

Chapter 4: Love

Getting Started: How do you know that someone loves you? How does mutual love look different from one-sided love?

1. How does prayer humble us? Why is humility a necessary part of love?

2. What kinds of work do you think of as especially important or especially difficult in the church? Read Colossians 4:12–13. What words do you notice that express Epaphras's effort as he prays? Why is prayer such hard work? What makes it so important?

3. What are some things we should pray together for the church as a whole (not just for individuals)? What should we pray for other churches? How would it encourage your church to know another church was praying for you?

4. In Matthew 5:44 Jesus tells us to pray for our enemies. Who are the enemies of God's people? Why do you think we often neglect to pray together for them?

5. We noted that text messaging and social-media platforms make it increasingly easy to ask people to pray *for us*, while conveniently distancing us from any obligation to pray *with them*. What are the problems with always asking for prayer for yourself (or your loved ones) without committing to joining others in mutual prayer?

6. How do we bear one another's burdens in prayer together? Are you willing to have others pray for you? Do you pray for others? Why is intercessory prayer especially loving when we are face-to-face with one another?

Further Study: Read 1 Thessalonians 5:23–26, Paul's prayer for the Thessalonian church.

- What things do Paul and his companions pray together for the Thessalonian believers in verses 23–24? How does the content of their prayer demonstrate love for that church?

- How is Paul's request in verse 25 also an expression of love? Of humility?

- How might Paul's exhortation in verse 26 relate to the previous verses?

Chapter 5: Discipleship

Getting Started: Think of someone who has had a large influence on your life. In what ways has his or her example shaped your actions, thinking, and desires?

1. In Luke 11:1 Jesus was praying, and one of his disciples requested, "Lord, teach us to pray." Why do you think he asked this? Who was the first person who taught you to pray? What did you learn then about prayer? What did you learn about God?

2. David Clarkson wrote, "In private [worship] you provide for your own good, but in public you do good both to yourselves and others." In what ways have other people done good to you by praying with you? What would you have missed if they had simply prayed privately?

3. What does it mean to:

- confess corporate sins as a community?
- confess individual sins corporately?
- confess individual sins individually?

When have you seen these practiced in your own church, community, or family?

4. When we pray together, how is repentance an antidote to pride?

5. Why is it important to understand that our desires can (and should) be trained? What standard do we use for our desires? If prayer is an expression of our desires, how does praying with other people help us to nurture right desires?

6. How does public thanksgiving glorify God? How does it do good to those praying with us? What opportunities do you have to give thanks to God in the hearing of others?

Further Study: Read 1 Samuel 2:1–10, the prayer of Hannah; and Luke 1:46–55, the praise of Mary.

- What were the circumstances of both Hannah's prayer and Mary's praise?

- List the words and phrases that these two prayers have in common. What other similarities do you notice?

- What do you learn from the prayers of Hannah and Mary? What other prayers in the Bible have taught you about the life of faith?

Chapter 6: Revival

Getting Started: When you hear the word *revival*, what first comes to your mind? Could you explain revival to a Christian friend, a non-Christian, or to a child?

1. J. I. Packer defined revival as "an extraordinary work of God the Holy Ghost reinvigorating and propagating Christian piety in a community." Why is it important to understand that revival is a corporate (and not just an individual) blessing?

- What is meant by "reinvigorating Christian piety in a community"? What do you think that might look like in your church?
- What is meant by "propagating Christian piety in a community"? What do you think that might look like in your town or city?
- Why is it important to have revival in the church as well as in the wider community? Is it possible to have one without the other? How might corporate revival relate to personal revival?

2. Read John 16:8; Romans 8:4, 26; Galatians 5:22–23; and Ephesians 5:18–19. How do these verses expand your understanding of what it means for a church or a community to grow in Christian piety?

3. Who is the author of revival? What is the difference between having faith in revival and having faith in God? Why is that distinction important?

4. How are missions and revival related? What encouragement do we have to pray together for the conversion of large numbers of people?

5. Read Luke 11:5–13. What encouragement(s) do we find in this passage regarding prayer? How could we apply this passage to praying together for revival?

Further Study: Read Psalm 85, a psalm of the sons of Korah.

- What is the congregation of God's people asking God to do?

- What did God do for them in the past? How does this compel and invigorate their request for the future? How can the church today pray on the basis of God's revival in the past?

- In this psalm, the congregation lists several specific characteristics of revival. What are they? Do we desire God to do those same things for us?

Chapter 7: Praying with the Church

Getting Started: List three things you do regularly with your church. Which of those is your favorite? Why? Which of those is the most important? Why?

1. In what two ways should our Lord's Day prayer with the church be "substantial"? Why? What does it mean to "pray until you pray"?

2. Why is leading in prayer the special duty and privilege of the elders? What would you say to someone who thinks that the elders lead in prayer because their prayers are better or more acceptable to God?

3. Why is it sometimes difficult to pray while someone else leads? What bad habits do you have during prayer in church? How can you seek to overcome them?

4. Why is it sometimes difficult to lead others in prayer? What bad habits do you have during prayer meetings? How can you seek to overcome those habits?

5. What are ways you could encourage your church to pray together?

Further Study: Read 2 Chronicles 6:12–42, Solomon's prayer of dedication.

- How does Solomon begin his prayer (vv. 14–15)? What can we learn from his introduction?

- List the petitions Solomon makes in his prayer on behalf of the people. How can we pray for similar things today?

- In what way was Solomon speaking as the voice of the entire assembly? What can you apply to your prayer as a congregation member? What can you apply as someone who leads others in prayer?

Chapter 8: Praying with Partners and Groups

Getting Started: Who are your closest friends? Why? What makes certain people great friends?

1. Read Daniel 2:17–19. In this passage Daniel asks his friends to pray with him. What makes friendship ideal for praying together? How have friendships led to praying together in your life? How has praying together deepened your friendships?

2. Read Colossians 4:3; 1 Thessalonians 3:10; 2 Thessalonians 3:1; and Philem. 22. What do you notice about Paul's requests? How do our personal prayer requests illuminate what is most important to us?

3. What kinds of requests do you typically pray about with others? What are some pitfalls we should avoid as we share requests? How would you like to pray in new ways after reading this chapter?

4. What is the relationship between scheduled prayer and spontaneous prayer? What keeps you from scheduled prayer? What keeps you from spontaneous prayer?

5. Dietrich Bonhoeffer wrote, "It is in fact the most normal thing in the common Christian life to pray together." To what extent has this been your experience? How could you make praying together "normal" in your life?

Further Study: Read Colossians 1:1–14, Paul and Timothy's prayer for the Colossians.

- What general characteristics describe this prayer?

- List the items they pray for the church. Do you pray that way with others for your own church and for other churches?

- Look at verses 3 and 9. What do you notice about *when* they pray? Could you say those things about your own prayer with others?

Chapter 9: Praying with Family and Guests

Getting Started: What is meant by "Home is where the heart is"? What do you love best about your home? If someone spent a day in your home, what would they learn about you?

1. Think about the suggestions in chapter 8 for praying with partners and groups. How could you apply these to praying in your home?

- Who could you pray with?
- What topics could you pray about?
- When and where could you pray?

2. Do you pray regularly with your spouse? From Scripture, how do we know this is important? Why is it sometimes difficult?

3. Read Matthew 19:13–15. How is this passage often misread? In what ways should we pray like those parents? How can this apply to every Christian who interacts with children?

4. Read Romans 12:13; Hebrews 13:2; and 1 Peter 4:9. What are we commanded to do and for whom? Why are we often quick to offer physical food but slow to offer spiritual nourishment in our homes?

5. Have you ever thought of prayer as an element of evangelism? What could a non-Christian learn from hearing you pray?

Further Study: Read Matthew 21:6–16, the children's praise.

- In verses 8–9 who is doing the praising? What about in verse 15? How did those children learn to pray? How did you learn to pray?

- What is Jesus's response to the children's praise? How can we as parents—and also as pastors, Sunday school teachers, and babysitters—encourage children to pray?

- In verses 10–11, who confronts spiritual truth as a result of hearing these praises? What about in verses 15–16? How can our family prayers be a testimony to others?

- Read Psalm 8:2. What is one of God's purposes in ordaining praise from the weakest members of his kingdom?

Conclusion

What circumstances or insecurities sometimes hinder you from praying with God's people? How can the example of others encourage you? How can meditating on Christ's presence overcome your reluctance? Relying on God's help, what resolutions do you have for praying together in the future?

Bibliography

Alexander, Eric J. *Prayer: A Biblical Perspective*. Carlisle, PA: Banner of Truth, 2012.

Alexander, James W. *Thoughts on Family Worship*. 1847. Reprint. Morgan, PA: Soli Deo Gloria, 1998.

Batterson, Mark. *The Circle Maker*. Grand Rapids, MI: Zondervan, 2011.

Bazely, Henry. "Standing at Prayer." In *Henry Bazely: The Oxford Evangelist, a Memoir*, by E. L. Hicks, 242–50. London: MacMillan, 1886.

Beale, G. K. *The Book of Revelation: A Commentary on the Greek Text*. New International Greek Testament Commentary. Grand Rapids, MI: Eerdmans, 1999.

Begg, Alistair. "Public Prayer: Its Importance and Scope (Part 1 of 2)." Message 1956 in *Household of Faith*, vol. 1. (MP3 podcast). *Truth for Life*. February 17, 2015.

Bickersteth, Edward. *A Treatise on Prayer: Designed to Assist in Its Devout Discharge*. Schenectady, NY: A. Van Santvoord & M. Cole, 1822.

Billings, J. Todd. *Union with Christ: Reframing Theology and Ministry for the Church*. Grand Rapids, MI: Baker Academic, 2011.

Bloomfield, Peter. *The Guide: Esther*. Auburn, MA: Evangelical Press, 2002.

Boice, James Montgomery. *Romans*. Vol. 2, *The Reign of Grace (Romans 5–8)*. Grand Rapids, MI: Baker, 1992.

Bonhoeffer, Dietrich. *Life Together*. 1954. Reprint, New York: Harper & Row, 1976.

The Book of Church Order of the Presbyterian Church in America. 6th. ed. Lawrenceville, GA: The Office of the Stated Clerk of the General Assembly of the Presbyterian Church in America, 2006.

Bradford, Eugene. *Intercessory Prayer: A Ministerial Task*. Boonton, NJ: Simpson, 1991.

Calvin, John. *Institutes of the Christian Religion*. Edited by John T. McNeill. Vols. 1 and 2. 1559. Reprint, Philadelphia: Westminster Press, 1960.

———. *John Calvin's Sermons on the Epistle to the Ephesians*. 1562. Reprint, Carlisle, PA: Banner of Truth, 1987.

Candlish, R. S. *An Exposition of Genesis*. 1868. Reprint, Wilmington, DE: Sovereign Grace, 1972.

Carson, D. A. *A Call to Spiritual Reformation: Priorities from Paul and His Prayers*. Grand Rapids, MI: Baker, 1992.

———. *The Gospel According to John*. Pillar New Testament Commentary. Grand Rapids, MI: Eerdmans, 1991.

Cashdollar, Charles D. *A Spiritual Home: Life in British and American Reformed Congregations, 1830–1915*. University Park, PA: Pennsylvania State University Press, 2000.

Catechism for Young Children: An Introduction to the Shorter Catechism. Reprint. Lawrenceville, GA: Christian Education & Publications, 2004.

Clarke, Samuel. *The Promises of Scripture, Arranged Under Their Proper Heads*. Liverpool, UK: Thomas Johnson, 1841.

Clarkson, David. "Public Worship to Be Preferred Before Private." In *The Practical Works of David Clarkson*. Vol. 3. Edinburgh: James Nichol, 1865.

The Confession of Faith Together with the Larger Catechism and the Shorter Catechism with Scripture Proofs. 3rd ed. Lawrenceville, GA: Christian Education & Publications, 1990.

Cryer, Neville B. "Biography of John Eliot." In *Five Pioneer Missionaries*. Edited by S. M. Houghton. Carlisle, PA: Banner of Truth, 1964.

Dickens, Charles. *Oliver Twist; or, The Parish Boy's Progress*. 3rd ed. Leipzig, Germany: Bernard Tauchnitz, 1843.

Doriani, Daniel M. *James*. Reformed Expository Commentary. Edited by Richard D. Phillips and Philip G. Ryken. Phillipsburg, NJ: P&R, 2007.

Edwards, Jonathan. *An Humble Attempt*. In *Works of Jonathan Edwards*. Vol. 5, *Apocalyptic Writings*. Edited by Stephen J. Stein. *WJE Online*, accessed December 26, 2014. http://edwards.yale.edu/archive?path=aHR0c DovL2Vkd2FyZHMueWFsZS5lZHUvY2dpLWJpbi9uZXdwaGlsbsby9nZ XRvYmplY3QucGw/Yy40OjUud2plbw==.

———. "Sermon Fifteen: Heaven is a World of Love." In *Works of Jonathan Edwards*. Vol. 8, *Ethical Writings*. Edited by Paul Ramsey. *WJE Online*, accessed October 8, 2014. http://edwards.yale.edu/archive?path=aHR0c DovL2Vkd2FyZHMueWFsZS5lZHUvY2dpLWJpbi9uZXdwaGlsbsby9nZ XRvYmplY3QucGw/Yy43OjQ6Q6MTUud2plbw==.

———. "Some Thoughts Concerning the Revival." In *Works of Jonathan Edwards*. Vol. 4, *The Great Awakening*. Edited by C. C. Goen. *WJE*

Online, accessed April 14, 2015. http://edwards.yale.edu/archive?path=
aHR0cDovL2Vkd2FyZHMueWFsZS5lZHUvY2dpLWJpbi9uZXddwaGl
sby9nZXRvYmplY3QucGw/Yy4zOjYud2d2d2j1d2d2plbw==.

Evans, Brad. "Some Incentives for Apocalyptic Prayer." Sermon, Presbyterian
Church of Coventry, Coventry, CT, June 9, 2002.

France, R. T. *The Gospel According to Matthew: An Introduction and Commentary.* Grand Rapids, MI: Eerdmans, 1985.

Heidelberg Catechism. In *Ecumenical Creeds and Reformed Confessions.*
Grand Rapids, MI: CRE, 1988.

Henry, Matthew. *Matthew Henry's Commentary.* Vol. 3, *Job to Song of
Solomon.* 1710. Reprint, Peabody, MA: Hendrickson, 1991.

Horton, Michael. *Ordinary: Sustainable Faith in a Radical, Restless World.*
Grand Rapids, MI: Zondervan, 2014.

Hulse, Erroll. *Give Him No Rest: A Call to Prayer for Revival.* Webster, NY:
Evangelical Press, 2006.

Humphrey, Heman. *Revival Sketches and Manual in Two Parts.* New York:
American Tract Society, 1859.

Johnson, Dennis E. *The Message of Acts in the History of Redemption.* Phillipsburg, NJ: P&R, 1997.

Johnson, Terry L. *The Family Worship Book: A Resource Book for Family
Devotions.* 1998. Reprint. Fearn, Ross-shire, UK: Christian Focus, 2009.

———. *Leading in Worship.* Oak Ridge, TN: Covenant Foundation, 1996.

Johnson, Terry L., and J. Ligon Duncan III. "Reading and Praying the Bible
in Corporate Worship." In *Give Praise to God: A Vision for Reforming
Worship.* Edited by Philip Graham Ryken, Derek W. H. Thomas, and J.
Ligon Duncan III. Phillipsburg, NJ: P&R, 2003.

Johnston, J. B. *The Prayer-Meeting and Its History, As Identified with the
Life and Power of Godliness, and the Revival of Religion.* Pittsburgh:
United Presbyterian Board of Publication, 1870.

Lamott, Anne. *Help, Thanks, Wow: The Three Essential Prayers.* New York:
Riverhead, 2012.

Leighton, Robert. *An Obedient and Patient Faith: An Exposition of 1st Peter.*
1693–1694. Reprint. Amityville, NY: Calvary Press, 1995.

Letham, Robert. *Union with Christ: In Scripture, History, and Theology.*
Phillipsburg, NJ: P&R, 2011.

Lloyd-Jones, D. Martyn. "Revival: An Historical and Theological Study."
In *Puritan Papers: Volume 2, 1956–1959.* Edited by D. M. Lloyd-Jones.
Phillipsburg, NJ: P&R, 2000.

———. *Studies in the Sermon on the Mount,* 2nd ed. Grand Rapids, MI:
Eerdmans, 1976.

Mack, Wayne A., and Dave Swavely. *Life in the Father's House: A Member's Guide to the Local Church*. Rev. ed. Phillipsburg, NJ: P&R, 2006.

Mackay, John L. *Isaiah. Vol. 2: Chapters 40–66*. EP Study Commentary. Carlisle, PA: EP Books, 2009.

Mandryk, Jason. *Operation World*, 7th ed. Downers Grove, IL: InterVarsity, 2010.

Manton, Thomas. *An Exposition on the Epistle of Jude*. 1658. Reprint, Minneapolis: Klock & Klock, 1978.

————. *James*. 1693. Reprint, Carlisle, PA: Banner of Truth, 1998.

M'Cheyne, Robert Murray. "Address: After the Communion." In *Memoir and Remains of the Rev. Robert Murray M'Cheyne, Minister of St. Peter's Church, Dundee*. By Andrew A. Bonar. Edinburgh: Oliphant, Anderson, & Ferrier, 1894.

————. "Evidence on Revivals: Answers to Queries on the Subject of the Revival in St. Peter's Parish, Dundee, Submitted to a Committee of the Presbytery of Aberdeen." In *Memoir and Remains*.

————. "Fourth Pastoral Letter: God the Answerer of Prayer." In *Memoir and Remains*.

The Memorial-Days of the Renewed Church of the Brethren. Ashton-under-Lyne, UK: T. Cunningham, 1822.

Miller, Samuel. *Thoughts on Public Prayer*. 1849. Reprint, Harrisonburg, VA: Sprinkle, 1985.

Moo, Douglas J. *The Letter of James: An Introduction and Commentary*. Grand Rapids, MI: Eerdmans, 1985.

Murray, Ian H. *Pentecost Today?: The Biblical Basis for Understanding Revival*. Cape Coral, FL: Founders Press, 1998.

Ogburn, Calvin. *The Young People's Prayer-Meeting and Its Improvement*. St. Louis, MO: Christian Publishing Company, 1894.

Packer, J. I. "Jonathan Edwards and the Theology of Revival." In *Puritan Papers. Vol. 2, 1960–1962*. Edited by J. I. Packer. Phillipsburg, NJ: P&R, 2001.

————. *Knowing God*. Twentieth Anniversary Edition. Downers Grove, IL: InterVarsity, 1993.

Packer, J. I., and Carolyn Nystrom. *Praying: Finding Our Way through Duty to Delight*. Downers Grove, IL: InterVarsity, 2006.

Pao, David W. *Thanksgiving: An Investigation of a Pauline Theme*. Downers Grove, IL: InterVarsity, 2002.

Payne, J. Barton. *1 and 2 Chronicles*. Expositor's Bible Commentary. Grand Rapids, MI: Zondervan, 1988.

Prime, Derek. *Practical Prayer*. 1986. Reprint, Ross-shire, UK: Christian Focus, 2007.

Prime, Samuel. *The Power of Prayer: The New York Revival of 1858*. 1859. Reprint, Carlisle, PA: Banner of Truth, 1991.

Reeves, Michael. *Delighting in the Trinity: An Introduction to the Christian Faith*. Downers Grove, IL: IVP Academic, 2012.

———. *Rejoicing in Christ*. Downers Grove, IL: IVP Academic, 2015.

Ryle, J. C. *Expository Thoughts on Luke*. Vol. 2. 1858. Reprint, Carlisle, PA: Banner of Truth, 2012.

Shakespeare, William. *Henry V*. In *The Gilbert Shakespeare: The Works of Shakespeare*. Edited by Howard Staunton. New York: George Rutledge & Sons, n.d.

Smith, Christian. *Soul Searching: The Religious and Spiritual Lives of American Teenagers*. Oxford, UK: Oxford University Press, 2005.

Spring, Gardiner. *Memoirs of the Rev. Samuel J. Mills, Late Missionary to the South Western Section of the United States, and Agent of the American Colonization Society, Deputed to Explore the Coast of Africa*. New York: New York Evangelical Missionary Society, 1820.

Thompson, Lewis O. *The Prayer Meeting and Its Improvement*. 5th ed. Chicago: Revell, 1878.

Tucker, Ruth A. *From Jerusalem to Irian Jaya: A Biographical History of Christian Missions*. Grand Rapids, MI: Zondervan, 1983.

Whitney, Donald S. *Spiritual Disciplines within the Church*. Chicago: Moody, 1996.

Young, Edward J. *The Book of Isaiah*. Vol. 3, *Chapters 40–66*. Grand Rapids, MI: Eerdmans, 1972.

Notes

Introduction

1. Dietrich Bonhoeffer, *Life Together* (1954; repr. New York: Harper & Row, 1976), 62.
2. Westminster Shorter Catechism, in *The Confession of Faith Together with the Larger Catechism and the Shorter Catechism with Scripture Proofs*, 3rd ed. (Lawrenceville, GA: Christian Education & Publications, 1990), Q&A 98. For those who are creed shy, this answer is simply a succinct summary of the Bible's teaching on prayer (see Pss. 32:5–6; 62:8; John 16:23; Phil. 4:6; 1 John 5:14).
3. J. I. Packer and Carolyn Nystrom, *Praying: Finding Our Way through Duty to Delight* (Downers Grove, IL: InterVarsity, 2006).
4. Ibid., 37.

Chapter 1: Relationship

1. Westminster Shorter Catechism, in *The Confession of Faith Together with the Larger Catechism and the Shorter Catechism with Scripture Proofs*, 3rd ed. (Lawrenceville, GA: Christian Education & Publications, 1990), Q&A 98.
2. Christian Smith, *Soul Searching: The Religious and Spiritual Lives of American Teenagers* (Oxford, UK: Oxford University Press, 2005), 148.
3. Anne Lamott, *Help, Thanks, Wow: The Three Essential Prayers* (New York: Riverhead, 2012), 1–2.
4. John Calvin, *Institutes of the Christian Religion*, ed. John T. McNeill, trans. Ford Lewis Battles (Philadelphia: Westminster Press, 1960), 3.20.12.
5. My father was in Dr. Clowney's class at Westminster Theological Seminary in Philadelphia in the 1970s.
6. The Bible frequently uses the word *covenant* to describe our relationship to a holy God. At its most basic, a covenant is a relationship that God defines, establishes, and guarantees.
7. J. Todd Billings, *Union with Christ: Reframing Theology and Ministry for the Church* (Grand Rapids, MI: Baker Academic, 2011), 25; emphasis original.
8. J. I. Packer, *Knowing God* (Downers Grove, IL: InterVarsity, 1993), 28.
9. Michael Reeves, *Delighting in the Trinity: An Introduction to the Christian Faith* (Downers Grove, IL: IVP Academic, 2012), 38.
10. Brad Evans, "Some Incentives for Apocalyptic Prayer," sermon, Presbyterian Church of Coventry, Coventry, CT, June 9, 2002.
11. D. A. Carson, *The Gospel According to John*, Pillar New Testament Commentary (Grand Rapids, MI: Eerdmans, 1991), 547.
12. Calvin, *Institutes*, 3.20.18.

13. James Montgomery Boice, *Romans*, vol. 2, *The Reign of Grace (Romans 5–8)* (Grand Rapids, MI: Baker, 1992), 981.

14. Michael Reeves, *Rejoicing in Christ* (Downers Grove, IL: IVP Academic, 2015), 32.

15. Robert Letham helpfully explains that "sons" here is not intended to ignore or marginalize the children of God who were created female. Instead, it is a testimony to each Christian's union with Christ; our designation as sons is a linguistic parallel, "pointing to our shared status with the Son of the Father." *Union with Christ: In Scripture, History, and Theology* (Phillipsburg, NJ: P&R, 2011), 54n19.

16. "God will either give you what you ask, or something far better." Robert Murray M'Cheyne, "Fourth Pastoral Letter: God the Answerer of Prayer," in Andrew A. Bonar, *Memoir and Remains of the Rev. Robert Murray M'Cheyne* (Edinburgh: Oliphant, Anderson, & Ferrier, 1894), 195.

17. We speak to God in our own words as unique persons "offering up . . . our desires unto God." We are not merely ventriloquist dummies or mute spectators to the divine conversation, but our awareness of the simultaneous divine conversation energizes and gives confidence to our prayer.

18. Reeves, *Delighting in the Trinity*, 98.

19. By "the church" we mean the people of God in all places and times. These people then gather together under biblical authorities in particular places, forming local churches.

20. Smith, *Soul Searching*, 147.

21. Charles D. Cashdollar, *A Spiritual Home: Life in British and American Reformed Congregations, 1830–1915* (University Park, PA: Pennsylvania State University Press, 2000), 59.

22. Jonathan Edwards, "Sermon Fifteen: Heaven Is a World of Love," in *Works of Jonathan Edwards*, vol. 8, *Ethical Writings*, ed. Paul Ramsey, *WJE Online*, accessed October 8, 2014, http://edwards.yale.edu/archive?path=aHR0cDovL2Vkd2FyZHMueWFsZS5lZHUvY2dpLWJpbi9uZXdwaGlsby9nZXRvYmplY3QucGw/Yy43OjQ6MTUud2plbw==.

23. Calvin, *Institutes*, 3.20.16.

Chapter 2: Duty

1. Praying together is often called "corporate prayer" because the church is a body, and *corpus* is the Latin word for "body." Corporate prayer is the prayer of the church, Christ's body.

2. D. Martyn Lloyd-Jones, *Studies in the Sermon on the Mount*, 2nd ed. (Grand Rapids, MI: Eerdmans, 1976), 307.

3. Neville B. Cryer, "Biography of John Eliot," in *Five Pioneer Missionaries*, ed. S. M. Houghton (Carlisle, PA: Banner of Truth, 1964), 203–17.

4. R. S. Candlish, *An Exposition of Genesis* (1868; repr. Wilmington, DE: Sovereign Grace, 1972), 76.

5. Edward J. Young, *The Book of Isaiah*, vol. 3, *Chapters 40–66* (Grand Rapids, MI: Eerdmans, 1972), 394.

6. See Peter Bloomfield, *The Guide: Esther* (Auburn, MA: Evangelical Press, 2002), 78.

7. John Calvin, *Institutes of the Christian Religion*, ed. John T. McNeill, trans. Ford Lewis Battles (Philadelphia: Westminster Press, 1960), 3.20.47.

8. J. C. Ryle, *Expository Thoughts on Luke*, vol. 2 (1858; repr. Carlisle, PA: Banner of Truth, 2012), 236.

9. See G. K. Beale, *The Book of Revelation: A Commentary on the Greek Text* (Grand Rapids, MI: Eerdmans, 1999), 930.

10. Westminster Shorter Catechism, in *The Confession of Faith Together with the Larger Catechism and the Shorter Catechism with Scripture Proofs*, 3rd ed. (Lawrenceville, GA: Christian Education & Publications, 1990), Q&A 98.

11. Beale, *Revelation*, 175; emphasis added.
12. E.g., in Acts 13:3; 15:40; 20:36–38; and 21:5–6 the believers gather together to pray on occasions of sending out men for missionary work. It is reasonable to assume that although prayer is not specifically mentioned at other departures, recorded in Acts 15:30, 33; 17:10, 14; 20:1, the church almost certainly prayed together.
13. Dennis E. Johnson, *The Message of Acts in the History of Redemption* (Phillipsburg, NJ: P&R, 1997), 5.
14. Rom. 12:12; 2 Cor. 1:11; Eph. 6:18; Phil. 4:5–6; Col. 4:2–4; 1 Thess. 5:16–18; 1 Thess. 5:25; 2 Thess. 3:1; 1 Tim. 2:1–2, 8; Heb. 13:18–19; James 5:13–16; Jude 20–21.

Chapter 3: Promise

1. D. Martyn Lloyd-Jones, *Studies in the Sermon on the Mount*, 2nd ed. (Grand Rapids, MI: Eerdmans, 1976), 309.
2. Tertullian, quoted in Thomas Manton, *An Exposition on the Epistle of Jude* (1658; repr. Minneapolis: Klock & Klock, 1978), 274.
3. John Calvin, *John Calvin's Sermons on the Epistle to the Ephesians* (1562; repr. Carlisle, PA: Banner of Truth, 1987), 677.
4. G. K. Beale, *The Book of Revelation: A Commentary on the Greek Text* (Grand Rapids, MI: Eerdmans, 1999), 456–57.
5. T. F. Torrence, quoted in Eric J. Alexander, *Prayer: A Biblical Perspective* (Carlisle, PA: Banner of Truth, 2012), 77.
6. Matthew Henry, *Matthew Henry's Commentary*, vol. 3, *Job to Song of Solomon* (1710; repr. Peabody, MA: Hendrickson, 1991), 365.
7. Jonathan Edwards, *An Humble Attempt*, in *The Works of Jonathan Edwards*, vol. 5, *Apocalyptic Writings*, ed. Stephen J. Stein, *WJE Online*, accessed December 26, 2014, http://edwards.yale.edu/archive?path=aHR0cDovL2Vkd2FyZHM ueWFsZS5lZHUvY2dpLWJpbi9zZXdpcGlsby9nZXRRvYmplY3QucGw/Yy40 OjUud2plbw==.
8. J. Barton Payne, *1 & 2 Chronicles*, Expositor's Bible Commentary (Grand Rapids, MI: Zondervan, 1988), 465.
9. See, e.g., R. T. France, *The Gospel According to Matthew: An Introduction and Commentary* (Grand Rapids, MI: Eerdmans, 1985), 276.
10. Tertullian, in *Exposition on the Epistle of Jude*, 274.
11. Mark Batterson, *The Circle Maker* (Grand Rapids, MI: Zondervan, 2011), 15.
12. Douglas J. Moo, *The Letter of James: An Introduction and Commentary* (Grand Rapids, MI: Eerdmans, 1985), 182.
13. Daniel M. Doriani, *James*, Reformed Expository Commentary, ed. Richard D. Phillips and Philip G. Ryken (Phillipsburg, NJ: P&R, 2007), 196.
14. Ibid.
15. Thomas Manton, *James*, Geneva Series of Commentaries (1693; repr. Carlisle, PA: Banner of Truth, 1998), 455.

Chapter 4: Love

1. Lewis O. Thompson, *The Prayer Meeting and Its Improvement*, 5th ed. (Chicago: Revell, 1878), 229.
2. The scope of this book doesn't allow us to examine the significant debate about physical posture in prayer. Theologians throughout church history have made well-reasoned, biblical arguments for particular postures, and churches derive their practice from the Scripture's teaching.
3. Thomas Manton, *James*, Geneva Series of Commentaries (1693; repr. Carlisle, PA: Banner of Truth, 1998), 455.

4. John Owen, quoted in Edward Bickersteth, *A Treatise on Prayer: Designed to Assist in Its Devout Discharge* (Schenectady, NY: A. Van Santvoord & M. Cole, 1822), 25.

5. J. B. Johnston, *The Prayer-Meeting and Its History, As Identified with the Life and Power of Godliness, and the Revival of Religion* (Pittsburgh: United Presbyterian Board of Publication, 1870), 267–68.

6. William Shakespeare, *Henry V*, in *The Gilbert Shakespeare: The Works of Shakespeare*, ed. Howard Staunton (New York: George Rutledge & Sons, n.d.), 4.3.62.

7. Wayne A. Mack and Dave Swavely, *Life in the Father's House: A Member's Guide to the Local Church*, rev. ed. (Phillipsburg, NJ: P&R, 2006), 214.

8. Prayer together also connects us to the church in all times. The prayers of long-ago saints may yet be answered in the church today, and our supplications may find their fulfillment in a generation still unborn.

9. Alistair Begg, "Public Prayer: Its Importance and Scope (Part 1 of 2)," Message 1956 in *Household of Faith*, vol. 1 (MP3 podcast), *Truth for Life*, February 17, 2015.

10. Johnston, *Prayer-Meeting*, 282–87.

11. Donald S. Whitney, *Spiritual Disciplines within the Church* (Chicago: Moody, 1996), 174; emphasis original.

12. Thompson, *Prayer Meeting*, 231.

13. Rom. 1:9–15; 15:23–24; 1 Cor. 16:7; Phil. 2:23–24; 1 Thess. 2:17, 3:10; 2 Tim. 1:4; cf. 3 John 14.

14. Rom. 16:16; 1 Cor. 16:20; 2 Cor. 13:12; 1 Thess. 5:26; cf. 1 Pet. 5:14.

15. Westminster Larger Catechism, in *The Confession of Faith Together with the Larger Catechism and the Shorter Catechism with Scripture Proofs*, 3rd ed. (Lawrenceville, GA: Christian Education & Publications, 1990), Q&A 147.

Chapter 5: Discipleship

1. Edward Bickersteth, *A Treatise on Prayer: Designed to Assist in Its Devout Discharge* (Schenectady, NY: A. Van Santvoord & M. Cole, 1822), 166.

2. David Clarkson, "Public Worship to Be Preferred Before Private," in *The Practical Works of David Clarkson*, vol. 3 (Edinburgh: James Nichol, 1865), 192.

3. Isaac Watts, quoted in Bickersteth, *Treatise on Prayer*, 168.

4. J. B. Johnston, *The Prayer-Meeting and Its History, As Identified with the Life and Power of Godliness, and the Revival of Religion* (Pittsburgh: United Presbyterian Board of Publication, 1870), 166.

5. Heidelberg Catechism, in *Ecumenical Creeds and Reformed Confessions* (Grand Rapids, MI: CRC, 1988), Q&A 129.

6. Samuel Miller, *Thoughts on Public Prayer* (1849; repr. Harrisonburg, VA: Sprinkle, 1985), 264.

7. John Calvin, *Institutes of the Christian Religion*, ed. John T. McNeill, trans. Ford Lewis Battles (Philadelphia: Westminster Press, 1960), 1.1.1.

8. Daniel M. Doriani, *James*, Reformed Expository Commentary, ed. Richard D. Phillips and Philip G. Ryken (Phillipsburg, NJ: P&R, 2007), 200. See also Thomas Manton, *James*, Geneva Series of Commentaries (1693; repr. Carlisle, PA: Banner of Truth, 1998), 459.

9. Erroll Hulse, *Give Him No Rest: A Call to Prayer for Revival* (Webster, NY: Evangelical Press, 2006), 142.

10. Westminster Larger Catechism, in *The Confession of Faith Together with the Larger Catechism and the Shorter Catechism with Scripture Proofs*, 3rd ed. (Lawrenceville, GA: Christian Education & Publications, 1990), Q&A 98.

11. Jonathan Edwards, *An Humble Attempt*, in *The Works of Jonathan Edwards*, vol. 5, *Apocalyptic Writings*, ed. Stephen J. Stein, *WJE Online*, accessed December 26, 2014, http://edwards.yale.edu/archive?path=aHR0cDovL2Vkd2FzHMueW

FsZS5lZHUvY2dpLWJpbi9uZXddwaGlssby9nZXRvYmplY3QucGcw/Yy40OjUud
2plbw==. For a helpful resource, see Samuel Clarke, *The Promises of Scripture,
Arranged under Their Proper Heads* (Liverpool, UK: Thomas Johnson, 1841).

12. David W. Pao, *Thanksgiving: An Investigation of a Pauline Theme* (Downers
Grove, IL: InterVarsity, 2002), 64.

Chapter 6: Revival

1. Samuel Prime, *The Power of Prayer: The New York Revival of 1858* (1859; repr.
Carlisle, PA: Banner of Truth, 1991), 3.

2. I am particularly indebted to Ian H. Murray's excellent book *Pentecost Today?:
The Biblical Basis for Understanding Revival* (Cape Coral, FL: Founders Press,
1988).

3. J. I. Packer, "Jonathan Edwards and the Theology of Revival," in *Puritan Papers:
vol. 2, 1960–1962*, ed. J. I. Packer (Phillipsburg, NJ: P&R, 2001), 33.

4. Jonathan Edwards called the Spirit "the chief of the blessings that are the subject
matter of Christian prayer." See Jonathan Edwards, *An Humble Attempt*, in *The
Works of Jonathan Edwards*, vol. 5, *Apocalyptic Writings*, ed. Stephen J. Stein,
WJE Online, accessed December 26, 2014, http://edwards.yale.edu/archive?path
=aHR0cDovL2Vkd2FyZHMueWFsZS5lZHUvY2dpLWJpbi9uZXdkwaGlssby9n
ZXRvYmplY3QucGcw/Yy40OjUud2plbw==. Also, cf. Matt. 7:11 ("How much
more will your Father who is in heaven give good things to those who ask him!")
with Luke 11:13 ("How much more will the heavenly Father give the Holy Spirit
to those who ask him!").

5. Murray, *Pentecost Today?*, 69; emphasis original.

6. Ibid., 18. Also, the Westminster Larger Catechism declares that the Spirit is present in every believer but does not always work "at all times, in the same measure." Westminster Larger Catechism, in *The Confession of Faith Together with
the Larger Catechism and the Shorter Catechism with Scripture Proofs*, 3rd ed.
(Lawrenceville, GA: Christian Education & Publications, 1990), 182.

7. Murray, *Pentecost Today?*, 17.

8. Charles Dickens, *Oliver Twist; or, The Parish Boy's Progress*, 3rd ed. (Leipzig,
Germany: Bernard Tauchnitz, 1843), 13.

9. Ibid.

10. Michael Horton, *Ordinary: Sustainable Faith in a Radical, Restless World* (Grand
Rapids, MI: Zondervan, 2014), 74–81.

11. Murray, *Pentecost Today?*, 78.

12. D. M. Lloyd-Jones, "Revival: An Historical and Theological Study," in *Puritan
Papers: vol. 2, 1956–1959*, ed. D. M. Lloyd-Jones (Phillipsburg, NJ: P&R, 2000),
318.

13. Packer, "Jonathan Edwards and the Theology of Revival," 37.

14. John L. Mackay, *Isaiah, vol. 2: Chapters 40–66*, EP Study Commentary (Carlisle,
PA: EP Books, 2009), 535.

15. Ibid., 536.

16. Jeremiah Lamphier, quoted in Prime, *Power of Prayer*, 7–8; emphasis original.

17. Ibid., 24. There were also daily noontime prayer meetings in Boston, Baltimore,
Washington, Richmond, Charleston, Savannah, Mobile, New Orleans, Vicks-
burg, Memphis, St. Louis, Pittsburgh, Cincinnati, and Chicago.

18. Ibid., 28–29.

19. Erroll Hulse, *Give Him No Rest: A Call to Prayer for Revival* (Webster, NY:
Evangelical Press, 2006), 8, 25.

20. Gardiner Spring, *Memoirs of the Rev. Samuel J. Mills, Late Missionary to the
South Western Section of the United States, and Agent of the American Coloni-
zation Society, Deputed to Explore the Coast of Africa* (New York: New York
Evangelical Missionary Society, 1820), 21.

21. Ibid., 29.
22. Ruth A. Tucker, *From Jerusalem to Irian Jaya: A Biographical History of Christian Missions* (Grand Rapids, MI: Zondervan, 1983), 122.
23. Heman Humphrey, *Revival Sketches and Manual in Two Parts* (New York: American Tract Society, 1859), 116.
24. J. B. Johnston, *The Prayer-Meeting and Its History, As Identified with the Life and Power of Godliness, and the Revival of Religion* (Pittsburgh: United Presbyterian Board of Publication, 1870), 162.
25. Ibid., 161; emphasis original.
26. Ibid., 165.
27. Ibid.
28. Ibid., 167.
29. Ibid., 165–66.
30. Ibid., 167.
31. Ibid., 166.

Chapter 7: Praying with the Church

1. In this chapter I use "church" in the more narrow sense of the local church: a body of believers and their children in a particular location under the leadership of ordained elders.
2. See, e.g., Eric J. Alexander, *Prayer: A Biblical Perspective* (Carlisle, PA: Banner of Truth, 2012), 76.
3. As I noted in chap. 4, the scope of this book doesn't allow us to examine the debate about posture in prayer.
4. See chap. 2: Duty, esp. 39–42.
5. Terry L. Johnson, *Leading in Worship* (Oak Ridge, TN: Covenant Foundation, 1996), 28.
6. Those individuals who are gifted, called, and ordained to authority in the local church. This includes the pastor and other elders.
7. Eugene Bradford, *Intercessory Prayer: A Ministerial Task* (Boonton, NJ: Simpson, 1991), 3–19.
8. Terry L. Johnson and J. Ligon Duncan III, "Reading and Praying the Bible in Corporate Worship," in *Give Praise to God: A Vision for Reforming Worship*, ed. Philip Graham Ryken, Derek W. H. Thomas, and J. Ligon Duncan III (Phillipsburg, NJ: P&R, 2003), 149.
9. Samuel Miller, *Thoughts on Public Prayer* (1849; repr. Harrisonburg, VA: Sprinkle, 1985), 131–76.
10. See chap. 4, "Love"; and chap. 5, "Discipleship."
11. Henry Bazely, "Standing at Prayer," in E. L. Hicks, *Henry Bazely: The Oxford Evangelist, a Memoir* (London: MacMillan, 1886), 247.
12. Edward Bickersteth, *A Treatise on Prayer: Designed to Assist in Its Devout Discharge* (Schenectady, NY: A. Van Santvoord & M. Cole, 1822), 11.
13. Derek Prime, *Practical Prayer* (1986, repr. Ross-shire, UK: Christian Focus, 2007), 119.
14. Miller, *Thoughts on Public Prayer*, 36.
15. For a fascinating (and sobering) historical survey of how multiplying church activities contributed to the nineteenth-century decline of the church prayer meeting, see Charles D. Cashdollar, *A Spiritual Home: Life in British and American Reformed Congregations, 1830–1915* (University Park, PA: Pennsylvania State University Press, 2000), 58–65.
16. Ibid., 59, 63.
17. It might make practical sense for a large church to hold several prayer meetings— one in each town or neighborhood where the members live—but each meeting should still be open to everyone.

18. Cashdollar, *Spiritual Home*, 59.
19. Miller, *Thoughts on Public Prayer*, 260–61.
20. D. Martyn Lloyd-Jones, *Studies in the Sermon on the Mount*, 2nd ed. (Grand Rapids, MI: Eerdmans, 1976), 322.

Chapter 8: Praying with Partners and Groups

1. Dietrich Bonhoeffer, *Life Together* (1954; repr. New York: Harper & Row, 1976), 62.
2. We will examine praying as families in the next chapter.
3. Samuel Prime, *The Power of Prayer: The New York Revival of 1858* (1859; repr. Carlisle, PA: Banner of Truth, 1991), 11.
4. "There can be no true prayer without these three." Robert Murray M'Cheyne, "Address after the Communion," in Andrew A. Bonar, *Memoir and Remains of the Rev. Robert Murray M'Cheyne* (Edinburgh: Oliphant, Anderson, & Ferrier, 1894), 459.
5. Westminster Shorter Catechism, in *The Confession of Faith Together with the Larger Catechism and the Shorter Catechism with Scripture Proofs*, 3rd ed. (Lawrenceville, GA: Christian Education & Publications, 1990), Q&A 98.
6. Voice of the Martyrs publishes maps, newsletters, apps, and emails to direct Christians to pray for the specific needs of the persecuted church worldwide. http://www.persecution.com.
7. Jason Mandryk, *Operation World*, 7th ed. (Downers Grove, IL: InterVarsity, 2010). This book helpfully organizes the nations and their prayer needs into a prayer guide for every day of the year.
8. *The Memorial-Days of the Renewed Church of the Brethren* (Ashton-under-Lyne, UK: T. Cunningham, 1822), 131.
9. Ibid., 138.
10. Ibid., 110.
11. Ibid., 123.
12. It is interesting to note how frequently children's and young people's prayer meetings were part of the church's life in earlier generations. Jonathan Edwards made a case for children's prayer meetings in his *Thoughts on Revival*; the children of the Moravians organized their own hourly prayer vigil; Robert Murray M'Cheyne reported that five of the thirty-nine prayer meetings in his town were "conducted and attended entirely by little children"; and at least one manual specifically for young people's prayer meetings was published in the nineteenth century. Contemporary Christianity could learn from this example. Surely if our children and teens would regularly pray together as they grow up, many of them would develop a lifelong practice of coming together to the Lord. This activity, so uncomfortable to attempt for the first time as an adult, would already be a familiar habit to those who had prayed often with their peers from the moment of their earliest lisping praise (Ps. 8:2).
13. Edward Bickersteth, *A Treatise on Prayer: Designed to Assist in Its Devout Discharge* (Schenectady, NY: A. Van Santvoord & M. Cole, 1822), 214.

Chapter 9: Praying with Family and Guests

1. James W. Alexander, *Thoughts on Family Worship* (1847; repr. Morgan, PA: Soli Deo Gloria, 1998), 2.
2. See chaps. 1–3.
3. Robert Leighton, *An Obedient and Patient Faith: An Exposition of 1st Peter* (1693–1694; repr. Amityville, NY: Calvary Press, 1995), 258.
4. See chap. 4, "Love."
5. D. A. Carson, *A Call to Spiritual Reformation: Priorities from Paul and His Prayers* (Grand Rapids, MI: Baker, 1992), 113–14.

6. Westminster Confession, in *The Confession of Faith Together with the Larger Catechism and the Shorter Catechism with Scripture Proofs*, 3rd ed. (Lawrenceville, GA: Christian Education & Publications, 1990), 21.6. Family worship usually includes more than just prayer. Singing, Bible reading, discussion and application of Scripture, and even catechism and Bible-memory training are all important elements. Other writers—notably J. W. Alexander and, more recently, Terry L. Johnson—have dealt comprehensively with the subject of family worship. Here, prayer will be our sole focus.

7. *Catechism for Young Children: An Introduction to the Shorter Catechism* (repr. Lawrenceville, GA: Christian Education & Publications, 2004), Q&A 19.

8. "But for the saints the occasion that best stimulates them to call upon God is when, distressed by their own need, they are troubled by the greatest unrest, and are almost driven out of their senses, until faith opportunely comes to their relief." John Calvin, *Institutes of the Christian Religion*, ed. John T. McNeill, trans. Ford Lewis Battles (Philadelphia: Westminster Press, 1960), 2.20.11.

9. *The Book of Church Order of the Presbyterian Church in America*, 6th. ed. (Lawrenceville, GA: Office of the Stated Clerk of the General Assembly of the Presbyterian Church in America, 2006), 56.5.

10. Terry L. Johnson, *The Family Worship Book: A Resource Book for Family Devotions* (1998; repr. Fearn, Ross-shire, UK: Christian Focus, 2009), 10.

11. Jonathan Edwards, "Some Thoughts Concerning the Revival," in *Works of Jonathan Edwards*, vol. 4, *The Great Awakening*, ed. C. C. Goen, *WJE Online*, accessed April 18, 2015, http://edwards.yale.edu/archive?path=aHR0cDovL2Vkd2 FyZHMueWFsZS5lZHUvY2dpLWJpbi9uZXdwaGlsby9nZXRvbmplY3QucGx0Gw /Yy4zOjYud2plbbw==.

12. See chap. 8, 108–11.

13. For many items on this list I am indebted to Alexander, *Thoughts on Family Worship*.

14. "This habitual, periodical, and mutual confession, morning and evening, of your mutual infirmities, your pride, your selfishness, your impatience, and your sinfulness, will have a great tendency also to soften down what is harsh and forbidding, and to unite you together." Edward Bickersteth, *A Treatise on Prayer: Designed to Assist in Its Devout Discharge* (Schenectady, NY: A. Van Santvoord & M. Cole, 1822), 162.

15. Alexander, *Thoughts on Family Worship*, 70.

Conclusion

1. J. B. Johnston, *The Prayer-Meeting and Its History, As Identified with the Life and Power of Godliness, and the Revival of Religion* (Pittsburgh: United Presbyterian Board of Publication, 1870), 209.

General Index

Scripture Index

THE GOSPEL **COALITION**

The Gospel Coalition is a fellowship of evangelical churches deeply committed to renewing our faith in the gospel of Christ and to reforming our ministry practices to conform fully to the Scriptures. We have committed ourselves to invigorating churches with new hope and compelling joy based on the promises received by grace alone through faith alone in Christ alone.

We desire to champion the gospel with clarity, compassion, courage, and joy—gladly linking hearts with fellow believers across denominational, ethnic, and class lines. We yearn to work with all who, in addition to embracing our confession and theological vision for ministry, seek the lordship of Christ over the whole of life with unabashed hope in the power of the Holy Spirit to transform individuals, communities, and cultures.

Through its women's initiatives, The Gospel Coalition aims to support the growth of women in faithfully studying and sharing the Scriptures; in actively loving and serving the church; and in spreading the gospel of Jesus Christ in all their callings.

Join the cause and visit TGC.org for fresh resources that will equip you to love God with all your heart, soul, mind, and strength, and to love your neighbor as yourself.

TGC.org

Also Available from the Gospel Coalition

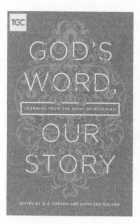

To see a full list of books published in partnership with the Gospel Coalition, visit crossway.org/TGC.